ORCHIDS
AS INDOOR PLANTS

ORCHIDS
AS INDOOR PLANTS

Brian and Wilma Rittershausen

Blandford Press
POOLE   DORSET

First published in the U.K. 1980

Copyright © 1980 Blandford Press Ltd
Link House, West Street
Poole, Dorset, BH15 1LL
Reprinted in this edition 1983

British Library Cataloguing in Publication Data

Rittershausen, Brian
  Orchids as indoor plants
  1. Orchid culture
  I. Title   II Rittershausen, Wilma
635.9'34'15   SB409

ISBN 0 7137 1303 8

Typeset in 11/12 pt Monophoto Ehrhardt by
Butler & Tanner Ltd,
Frome and London.

CONTENTS

The authors wish to express their sincere thanks to the following for the use of photographs in this book: Eric Crichton, Alan Greatwood, Robin Fletcher, The Orchid Review Ltd, and Vacherot and Lecoufle.

INTRODUCTION

The orchid family is one of the largest and most successful in the whole plant kingdom. Orchids have colonised almost the entire globe and species can be found growing wild in every continent with the exception of Antarctica. Their habitats range from sea level to the snowline on the highest mountains, from dry arid deserts to hot steaming jungles, and from the mellow downs of England to the steppes of Siberia. Individual plants have evolved into many forms to cope with whatever conditions these environments may provide. These are the species, the naturally occurring wild flowers of the world, designed by nature over millions of years to survive in a thousand and one different habitats. Many of these plants are highly specialised and it is extremely difficult to recreate the conditions they require under cultivation. Also, many of them produce small and often unattractive flowers, rendering them of interest only to the botanists. Many botanical books have been written describing these species, but here they are mentioned only briefly to enable the reader to understand that of this huge family of plants, only a very small percentage are showy and colourful and it is these varieties which have caught the imagination of the grower from earliest times. Even today, while we know so much about the planet we live on, botanists are still classifying new and previously undiscovered species. The total number of orchid species can only be estimated, and varies considerably from one authority to another. The figure of 25,000 is universally accepted as a conservative estimate.

Wild orchids
The vast majority of the tropical orchids have evolved a method of growing upon the branches and trunks of forest trees. These species are known as epiphytes or 'air plants', which should not be confused with

7

parasites which actually live off the trees. Orchids merely use the tree as anchorage and a means of support to enable them to reach the air and light. They use their host, not to extract food, but as a ladder over which they climb, their strong aerial roots clinging to the bark or hanging suspended in the air. As long as the forest tree stands, the orchids growing on it are safe. Their life span in nature is therefore directly related to the life span of the host tree. Apart from the humidity rising from the forest floor which is so important to their welfare, the orchids find sufficient nourishment to satisfy their meagre needs from the decaying vegetation which collects in the axils of the branches and around their own roots, which sometimes form huge mats for this purpose.

The epiphyte orchids are among the easiest varieties to cultivate under artificial conditions and nearly all the hybrids which we grow today are descended from species of the tropical or sub-tropical regions of the earth. There are, however, many thousands of orchids which grow as terrestrials. These are the plants which grow in the ground at the edge of forests or in open grasslands where the competition with other, larger growing plants is not so great. Terrestrial orchids are particularly abundant in the colder climates where their subterranean bulbs and roots are protected against the harsh winters. Many different varieties are to be found in North America and Europe.

Hybrids
Over the past ten decades, growers have attempted to cultivate most species of orchid from time to time. The Victorians were the first generation to build greenhouses especially to accommodate tropical plants and to import the orchid species from the tropical regions of the world. The most beautiful and showy of these were regarded as the finest flowers in the world, and it was not long before our forefathers succeeded in crossing the different species. The results were astonishing and within a few years completely different forms appeared. These crossings of two species are called hybrids. The first man-made hybrids were then crossed with each other to produce even more amazing plants which combined the features of the species. Years of dedicated selective breeding led to the modern hybrid, which often bears no resemblance at all to the original species from which it started, but outshines the wild varieties with its flamboyant beauty and form.

Commercial propagation
Anyone who becomes involved with the breeding of exquisite orchids from seed soon finds that a fertile seed pod may produce tens of thousands

8

of minute seeds, all so small that they are easily carried on the wind and in this way distributed far and wide in their natural state. This output may seem extravagant but as very few of these will land in exactly the right place to germinate and grow, a high productivity is essential to ensure survival of the species. Just as very few acorns grow into mighty oaks, so, in nature, very few orchid seeds ever get started.

The early hybridisers found cross pollination of orchids an easy procedure once the basic structure of the orchid flower had been realised. Their problems commenced with the germination of the extremely fine seed. Unlike the acorn which can be grown quite easily with a little encouragement and has its own built-in food reserve upon which the young growing plant can rely for its initial supply of nourishment, the orchid seed has no such reserve. Although the early hybridisers sowed tens of thousands of orchid seeds, they were lucky if they succeeded in germinating a mere ten plants! The reason for this was not immediately apparent until the botanical scientists came to the aid of the growers. It was discovered that the orchid seed could only germinate in association with a microscopic root fungus which initiated the growth of the seed. With this discovery it became possible to analyse the various chemicals and trace elements released by the fungus and to produce a synthetic mixture which was acceptable to the orchid seed. When seeds were sown in sterile flasks on an agar-based medium containing this mixture, the results were dramatic. This technique revolutionised hybridisation and the raising of orchid seedlings passed from the greenhouse to the laboratory.

Today, this method remains the only commercial way of producing orchid plants by seed and it is now possible to germinate just about every seed that is sown. Briefly, the solution containing the precise amounts of ingredients is poured into glass bottles and allowed to set to a jelly. The orchid seed is then spread evenly over the surface of the jelly and the bottle is tightly stoppered. Within nine to ten months, depending upon the variety, each plant will have produced leaves and roots. At this stage they can be removed and grown in conventional compost in special seedling houses. Like all young life they need constant care and attention to ensure that they continue to grow and reach maturity. With orchids this may be a matter of three to four, or as many as seven, years.

The other major method of propagation used by commercial growers, is a modern technique known as meristemming. Whereas raising orchids from seed produces new varieties and hybrids, meristem culture gives rise to unlimited quantities of plants identical to one parent plant. This remarkable process is achieved in the laboratory by taking a single cell,

9

or group of cells, from the centre of a new growth under sterile conditions and cultivating them until a quantity of green tissue is produced. When divided and cultured on agar jelly, this tissue eventually grows into individual plants which can then be grown on to maturity in the normal way. The great advantage of this method is that unlimited identical orchids can be produced in far less time than would be taken by conventional propagation. For the amateur, meristemming means that top quality plants are made available at reasonable prices with the variety guaranteed.

Having attained adult size, the plants will continue to grow and flower on an annual cycle for an indefinite number of years, provided that they are given the encouragement to do so. The life span of an orchid is, in theory, endless. They never die of old age, and are only killed by accident or misunderstanding of their needs. Adult plants eventually become large enough to be divided into two or more plants, and the oldest bulbs can be removed singly for propagation to increase the stock. For convenience, growers tend to divide plants in their care to keep them down to a manageable size, or to exchange pieces with friends. In the wild, species growing undisturbed can grow into enormous clumps several feet across, possibly hundreds of years old. Apart from man, who destroys their environment, they have few natural enemies.

Orchid availability
The potential orchid grower has a far greater choice than is available with any other flower, and selection can be made from an almost endless range of varying types to bloom throughout the year. Today these plants are mostly hybrids, but it was not always so. In past decades the newcomer to orchids was encouraged to make his or her first purchases from inexpensive species. These were wild plants which had been collected from the tropical jungles. Upon arrival at commercial establishments they would be hurriedly potted and immediately offered for sale and, owing to their low cost, beginners would be tempted to buy them to start their orchid collections. However, newly imported plants are in an unfit state for the inexperienced grower: their roots have probably been damaged or destroyed during transit and the chances of survival under amateur care are very slight. Establishing and acclimatising orchid plants from the wild is a skilled job which is best left to the experts who know how to treat the ailing plants to get them back into a state of good health. New roots have to be speedily encouraged and shrivelled pseudo bulbs must be plumped up before a plant can start to grow and be in perfect health for sale to the beginner.

10

The 'import, pot and sell' attitude enabled the dealer to offer an enormous range of orchid species at ridiculously low prices. Many of the plants were bought merely for their flowers and were discarded when their blooming period was over. This unfortunate trade which continued for many years has now largely ceased. What seemed an inexhaustible supply of orchid species from the vast regions of India as well as Central and South America is finally coming to an end as the rapid spread of agriculture and the lumber industry in these newly developing countries decimates the natural habitat of both fauna and flora. New laws, designed to save the remaining wild orchids, have been passed which require strict licensing of the export and import of orchid species. This has seen the decline of the dealer who imported cheap orchid species with a view to 'getting rich quick'.

The reputable firms which have remained in business are permitted to import limited quantities of specific orchid species under licence, while at the same time they increase their stock by propagation and by raising plants from seed. This ensures that stronger and healthier nursery plants of the most beautiful and popular species remain in cultivation. No longer will they be sold far below their value for a quick profit. These plants are grown for four to five years before reaching maturity and being offered for sale as flowering sized plants. The high production costs and years of work involved mean that the species can cost more to produce than the sturdier, man-made hybrids. Although hybrids are the result of many years of selective breeding using only the very best and robust species to start with, the extra vigour inherited has enabled the commercial grower to reduce time and costs in producing plants for sale. The modern, free blooming and vigorous, compact hybrid with its built-in adjustable tolerance to suit a variety of habitats will be far more satisfactory to the hobbyist in the long run than the more delicate species. The modern hybrid stands out as a triumph to those growers who had the foresight to combine all the best qualities of a number of different species.

While the range of species available to the grower has greatly diminished, the choice of hybrids has increased beyond the wildest imagination of our forefathers. Those species which have been in cultivation for some years will satisfy the connoisseurs and the serious collectors of the world's wild orchids, who have the ideal conditions under which to cultivate and preserve them, but they should not be attempted as house plants. Constantly improving cultural techniques being refined by the nurseryman ensures that he will provide an ever increasing range of colourful hybrids to supply the demand for house plants.

11

The orchid plant
Most of the orchids which are suitable for indoor culture consist of a number of pseudo bulbs, or false bulbs. These are basically swollen stems used as a means of storing water; they vary in size and shape and also in the number of leaves carried. For example, Cymbidiums produce rounded pseudo bulbs with an average of ten long, narrow leaves on each, whereas Cattleyas have elongated pseudo bulbs which carry only one or two thick, fleshy leaves. One (or more) new pseudo bulb is produced during each growing season and it is attached to the previous one by a rhizome. The rhizome is usually underground but in Cattleyas it is clearly visible on the surface. Roots are produced by each pseudo bulb at the beginning of the growing season when the young growth is developing.

A healthy evergreen plant should consist of a group of hard, plump pseudo bulbs, most of which carry leaves, with some older leafless bulbs. The deciduous types have only one or two pseudo bulbs in leaf at a time.

Not all orchids recommended for indoor culture produce pseudo bulbs; some are bulbless. Paphiopedilums consist of a number of growths and a good plant can have several growths at any time. Another method of growth is shown by Phalaenopsis which produce leaves from an upward growing rhizome, or main stem, from which they also flower.

The orchid flower, although very diverse in shape and colouring, always conforms to a basic structure, comprising three outer sepals and three inner petals. Usually there are two equal lateral petals and one lower petal which is modified into the lip or pouch. The lip is commonly the most beautiful or eye-catching part of the flower because it is designed to attract the pollinating agent—usually an insect. The central structure of the orchid flower is called the column, and contains both male and female parts. The pollen is carried in small masses at the tip of the column.

PART I

Choosing Orchids for the Home

In Part II, we examine the different conditions which exist within the home, from the garden room with its sunny light environment, to the warm humid bathroom, kitchen and living room. Each of these areas provides different conditions in which orchids can be acclimatised and will thrive. It is of little use trying to grow a sun loving plant in a dark corner, or an orchid which originates from areas of dense shade in a position where it will suffer the glare of the midday sun. First consideration, when choosing orchids, must be given to the area in which you intend to grow your plants, and then look for the varieties which are most suited, rather than the other way around. Having bought a beautiful plant in flower it is disappointing to find that there is nowhere in the home where it will flourish. This inevitably means that as soon as it has finished flowering it can only deteriorate and sooner or later be consigned to the dustbin. This, of course, happens to many pot plants and may be acceptable to the individual who is prepared to purchase live plants and discard them when they have finished blooming in the same way that one would throw away a wilted bunch of flowers. Each year thousands upon thousands of flowering plants such as cyclamen and azaleas are purchased simply for the short period they are in bloom, only to be discarded when they are considered no longer beautiful. This, of course, has been taken into consideration by the nurserymen who raise them, by the garden centres who sell them, and by the customers who purchase them. While there is little to commend this wasteful production, it satisfies a need and provides

13

much short term pleasure to many people, but in no way can it be termed *growing* plants.

The object of this book is to encourage the home orchid grower, the person who wishes to succeed with orchids as house plants, growing them for many years as healthy, flowering plants under the unnatural conditions of the home. The orchids become not only an attractive display, but also a fascinating and inspiring hobby providing the grower with the pleasure and excitement of having grown and flowered his own plants year after year.

When choosing orchids, always obtain the very best plants you can afford. While orchids are sold at many different prices, the cheapest will be young plants which will require growing on for a number of years before they reach flowering size and maturity. Growing orchids as house plants requires that the plants should be flowering size when purchased to ensure that you get the best value and a good show of flowers in their first season. The house is not the best place in which to grow young, immature plants. The larger and stronger plants, while requiring a higher initial outlay, will be the most rewarding. Also, they will adjust more readily to the varying conditions of the house having their own reserves to rely upon while they adjust themselves. In this way they will continue to grow and flower regularly and the grower will be rewarded with a fine display of flowers. Small plants and propagations do not look so attractive or create an eye-catching display. For this reason the house orchids are at their best when allowed to grow on into large specimen plants. They should only require dividing when they become too large to handle comfortably. While some orchids can be continually divided about every two or three years, if room permits they will look far more beautiful when left as one plant. It will be necessary from time to time to remove a number of back bulbs when they cease to benefit the plant. While these may be easily propagated from and one's stock of the plant increased, it must be remembered that these propagations will take up to five years or even longer indoors to reach maturity. During this time they will take up valuable space which could be occupied by other, flowering orchids. It is simply a matter of choice whether one fills the available space with all flowering plants, or young, non-producing plants.

All the same, while the aim should be to fill one's house with flowering plants, there is nothing to compare with the thrill of raising one's own plants. If there is another room or special area where young plants and propagations can be raised, one may feel it is worth the time and work involved. These young plants will require far more attention than the

14

mature plants and may take longer to reach flowering size than they would do in a greenhouse. Before purchasing young stock, it may be advisable to remove a few back bulbs from your existing stock, so that you can try your hand at growing young plants with no further outlay. If this is unsuccessful, only time has been wasted.

Orchid names

While this book does not deal with the botanical classification of all the different orchids, it is necessary to explain a little of how these plants are grouped, as many of them are known only by their latin names, and the potential grower will have to learn to cope with catalogues which may consist of page after page of latin names.

Briefly, closely related plants are grouped into different genera. From the classification point of view each genus consists of a handful of naturally occurring species, or a hundred or so closely related plants. Examples of different genera are: *Paphiopedilum*, *Cymbidium*, *Cattleya* and *Odontoglossum*. Originally, these genera contained only the natural species, but with the development of interbreeding, man-made hybrids have been introduced. From the way the name of the plant is written it is possible to tell whether it is a species or a hybrid. For example, *Paphiopedilum insigne* is a species, while *Paphiopedilum* Geelong is a hybrid. The second name of the hybrid is written in roman type and with a capital first letter, while the second name of the species is in italics, has a small initial and is latinised.

Many growers do not feel inclined to bother with remembering the names of the plants which they grow only for pleasure and, indeed, may have given them their own nicknames by which they remember them! If this is as far as the interest in your plants goes, then their classification can be of little importance. However, should you wish to find out more about the plants you have taken into your care, why they grow as they do, why they are a certain shape, their flowering habits and origins, then a label is the first thing you need. Armed with the name of your plant you can soon look up the relevant information regarding it, or seek the help and advice of an expert. Having acquired a basic understanding of the names of your orchids and those related to them, you can pick up any commercial catalogue and read through the names without being totally confused. So much is lost to you by not knowing the names of your plants, while a little learning will open up the whole of the orchid world.

In the following pages we have not placed the orchids under discussion in any order of preference or recommendation; as we will see in Part II,

15

so much depends upon where you plan to grow them. For the person with a choice of several situations it may be possible to grow a number of varieties which will not live together. The plants have been divided into their various genera, with a discussion on the best place to grow them and listing the most suitable species or hybrids to grow. Generally, the beginner would be best advised to acquire hybrids wherever possible. Nowadays many hybrids have been bred especially for the purpose of growing in the home. These have a different kind of vigour which makes them much more adaptable and able to survive without the specialised conditions required by many of the species. However, this does not mean that all species are unsuitable.

Pleiones
These are the coolest growing of all the cultivated orchids and will succeed without any artificial heating. They should be kept on a cool window sill or even in an unheated, frost free conservatory. The minimum night temperature can drop for short periods to a few degrees above freezing, while they can tolerate summer daytime temperatures into the mid 20s°C (70s°F).

The plants are small, producing a compact growth. Round or oval shaped pseudo bulbs are produced which carry a single green leaf during the growing season. The bulbs are up to 5 cm (1–2 in.) high and are completed during the summer growing season. In the autumn the single leaf is shed, having first become spotted with age and then turned yellow. From this time until new growth is seen in the spring no water is required by the plant, which has become dormant. With the lengthening of the days the new growth will commence; water should then be given, and within a short time the plant will bloom. A single flower bud emerges from the centre of the young growth and the delicate flower will last for about ten days. Each year after flowering the bulbs should immediately be repotted. This will allow the new roots being made at this time to take full advantage of the fresh compost and will avoid any damage which may occur if the roots are left to grow too long before repotting. The two-year-old bulbs which are shrivelled and obviously dead should be removed, leaving only last year's green, healthy bulbs with their adjoining new growths. The rooting system is not extensive, and the bulbs should be potted into shallow pans rather than deep pots. These pans will vary according to the number of bulbs in a pan, but may start at 7 cm (3 in.). Each bulb should be allowed about 2 cm (1 in.) of space between it and the next bulb. The compost should consist of sphagnum peat and sand

16

with a little hoof and horn added to the base. The bulbs must sit on top of the compost, and not be buried. The summer is the growing season when the new bulb is forming and during this time the compost should not be allowed to become dry. The plants should be kept in a cool, shady place until the leaves have been shed, when they should be removed to a position of full light.

There are very few hybrids generally available among the Pleiones; the species are extremely popular because they are easy to grow, propagate rapidly, and are the least expensive. *Pleione formosana* is the most popular. Its bulbs are dark green or purple, and the flowers a soft, delicate pink with a large frilled lip which is dotted and lined in yellow and light brown. There is also the white form, *P. formosana* var. *alba*, whose only colour is a light yellowing in the lip. *P. humilus* carries slightly smaller white flowers, the lip prettily streaked in red lines. All these species bloom in the early spring, *P. humilus* usually first. A word of warning here: while the above varieties can be easily and successfully grown by the beginner, other varieties are not nearly so easy to start with and these are not to be recommended. *P. pracox* and *P. forestii* require much more specialised conditions and a better knowledge of their requirements.

The Pleiones come from China and the island of Formosa. Today you can buy bulbs which have been cultivated in nurseries for a number of years and are not imported. You should expect to buy the bulbs already potted and established, although imported bulbs are still sometimes sold bare root.

Paphiopedilums

These are the well known and popular 'lady's slipper' orchids, so named because the lip has developed into a large pouch resembling a slipper. They were among the first orchids to be cultivated as house plants and were a common sight in the Wardian Cases of Victorian drawing rooms. In older books you will find them referred to as Cypripediums. This large group of orchids was later divided, and the Cypripediums of the modern classification are quite unsuitable as house plants, as well as being difficult to obtain; many are extremely rare plants indeed.

Paphiopedilum species are widely distributed throughout the Far East, stretching from China and the Himalayas in the far north to the islands of the Philippines, all the way down to Malaya and south to New Guinea. The species are usually terrestrial in habit, growing in the ground among other shady vegetation. Occasionally some may be found growing as epi-phytes on the lower branches of trees. Unlike most orchids, the plants

17

do not have pseudo bulbs but produce growths, each consisting of five or six leaves. New growths are added each year and are joined together by an underground rhizome. The colour of the leaves may vary considerably; some being plain dark green while others have a red or mauve flecking at the base and on the undersides of the foliage. Other types are mottled all over in a contrasting light and dark pattern. It is this beautiful foliage which makes these orchids particularly attractive as foliage plants all the year round.

Their flowers are extremely long lasting often remaining for eight to ten weeks in perfection, and this is one reason why they were among the first orchids to be hybridised. So successful has this been that today the hobbyist can choose from an enormous range of types and colours. Some typical varieties produce a single bloom on a long stem, while others of different descent will give three or four flowers on a spray. Further varieties will bloom in succession producing a number of flowers over a period of twelve months, remaining nearly always in bloom. Paphiopedilums are so popular as house plants, particularly in Europe, that vast quantities are produced by nurserymen in an almost unlimited range of colours, shapes and sizes. The flowering period is mainly during the winter months, although with new varieties continually appearing on the market, it is possible, with careful selection, to have blooms all the year round.

For indoor growing, the beginner should start with mature, flowering sized plants, and not be tempted to immediately start trying to divide and propagate the plants until considerable experience has been gained. The full beauty of these orchids often cannot be realised until they are specimen plants which have been allowed to grow on for several years without continued division. These specimen plants will produce several flowers each year from the new growths, providing months of bloom.

Generally, the green leaved varieties require slightly cooler conditions than the heavily mottled varieties, although it is not impossible to grow them together with careful attention to the temperature. As shade loving plants they should never be exposed to bright sunlight and should not be grown on a very sunny window sill unless they are fully protected from the fiercest sun in the summer months. Their delicate foliage can easily become scorched by sun through glass.

The Paphiopedilums make ideal plants for an orchid case; their size is easily accommodated, and they will benefit from the fairly constant temperature between summer and winter, day and night. Because they are continuously growing and do not have a resting period they enjoy fairly warm, comfortable conditions all the year round. In the orchid case they will be fully protected from cold draughts and from bright sunlight.

Since they do not possess pseudo bulbs, their only food reserve is held in the fleshy leaves and thick roots. Consequently, they should not be allowed to become dry at any time. The compost should be kept evenly moist, and it is important that the compost be open and very well drained to avoid saturation and damage to the root system. The plants should be kept clean and free from dust by regular sponging of the leaves, although direct spraying is to be avoided. The plants like to be grown in as small a pot as possible, and repotted only when necessary; about every second or third year.

The modern hybrid will have several different species in its background, bringing together the various qualities the species have to offer, and producing a plant quite unlike anything found in nature. All the species are extremely decorative plants, and were every bit as popular as the larger and more flamboyant hybrids until about a decade ago. Since that time most of these well loved species are no longer available, owing to abuse in the form of overcollecting, and the spread of agriculture which destroys their native habitat. Another contributory factor is the new conservation laws which have recently come into force in an attempt to protect the species which remain in the wild. The loss of the species in cultivation has led to a greater demand for the hybrids which in many cases are far better suited to cultivation indoors. With the combined qualities which have been bred into the hybrids the result is a stronger and more vigorous plant which has a built-in tolerance to artificial conditions. For this reason no Paphiopedilum species is recommended for the beginner to start with, but they are mentioned where they have had influence in the making of the hybrids. Also, very few hybrids have been mentioned by name. It must be remembered that thousands of hybrids exist and it would be misleading and pointless to give a list of names. Instead we have mentioned *lines* of breeding, and the species which have made them possible, to give the reader an insight to the types which are available. Paphiopedilums are the only orchids among the most popular varieties that cannot be raised by the mass propagation method known as meristemming. This means that all the plants which are available have been produced by seed or conventional propagation by division.

Among the hybrids are the well loved types which produce large, well rounded flowers of a heavy texture, with spotted dorsal petals and highly glossed petals and pouches. These come in a variety of colours from lime green and clear yellow to rich dark reds and bronzes with any number

19

of shades in between and various spots and stripes. These are the types which, although many times removed from the species, can be traced back through their pedigree to *Paphiopedilum insigne* and its many varieties (including the yellow form *P. insigne* var. *sanderae*), and also *P. bellatulum*. It was the combination of these two completely different Paphiopedilums which formed the base for the modern breeding lines.

P. insigne originates from the Himalayas. It is a green leaved species, with slender foliage. The flowers are carried singly on tall, slender stems and last for many weeks during the winter. The flowers are greeny/

Paphiopedilum Hellas. Plants with these heavy, well rounded blooms flower mainly throughout the winter, when they are extremely long lasting. Note development from bud to fully opened flower, and staked bloom.

bronze, the dorsal petal white, shading to green at the base and spotted with brownish purple. The variety *sanderae* is pure yellow throughout, which provided the hybridisers with a completely different colour line for breeding. The main contributions of this species to the early hybrids were colouring and length of stem.

P. bellatulum, which comes from Thailand, represents a different group within this genus, and produces small, neat growths with beautifully marbled foliage. The leaves are thick and brittle; easily snapped like a young carrot. The flowers are produced from an exceedingly short stem and 'sit' neatly on top of the diminutive foliage. These blooms, which are produced singly, are perfectly round in shape and coloured a soft powdery white with heavy, dark red spotting. When crossed with *P. insigne* it passed its rounded shape to the hybrids.

Other species which have played a part in producing the range of colourations, shapes of flower and lengths of stem available amongst the Paphiopedilum hybrids, are *P. spicerianum, villosum* and *fairrieanum*. From the smaller growing *P. niveum*, which comes from Thailand and Malaysia and produces dainty, well rounded white flowers on a medium stem, have come a host of white and pastel hybrids with delicate spotting or flushing.

Paphiopedilum Maudiae. *This hybrid carries beautiful, mottled foliage and the flower on a slender stem is apple green with a white, green-striped dorsal petal. One of the longest lasting flowers.*

The mottled leaved Paphiopedilums give a different type of flower, having been produced from a different range of species. The mottled leaved types are noted for their lighter, more open flower. These are carried singly on a tall slender stem, the dorsal being large and vertically striped, while the narrower petals are generally more vertical, embracing the pouch. An important species in this group is *P. callosum* and its coloured forms. This lovely species from Thailand has everything to commend it. The graceful flowers are green and purple, and the dorsal is white, flamed with purple. From this and several related species comes a further range of hybrids, where selective breeding has given rise to many different colours, including clear apple green through red and purple in rich hues.

21

These mottled leaved types are also extremely long lasting, and will bloom freely throughout the year.

A further group of Paphiopedilums comes from the Philippines and has produced the unique varieties which give the multiflowering stems with three to four flowers on a spray. These flowers are more slender in shape, with longer and narrower petals, and the dorsal petal is usually smaller than in the more conventional types. These hybrids are less in number and often do not go back through so many generations. This means that the resemblance to the original species is more noticeable and the colourings are more subtle, being represented by pink, beige and light green or brown. Two species which have helped to produce these unusual hybrids are *P. philippinense* and *P. haynaldianum* both from the Philippines. *P. philippinense* produces several striking blooms, richly coloured in dark purple. The petals are long, narrow and often twisted along their length. They extend to well below the pouch. *P. haynaldianum* is lightly coloured in green and pink. Several large flowers are well spaced along a tall stem, the dorsal and pouch are small while the petals are elongated, and adorned with spots toward the centre of the flower. *P. chamberlainianum* is a related species which comes from Malaysia and produces numerous blooms one at a time in a succession which will continue for twelve months or more. Recent breeding from this species and its various coloured forms is producing yet another range of alternative hybrids which have slightly smaller flowers, more compact in shape and showing green and pink or yellow in their colouring. These flowers are often adorned with short hairs along the crest of the petals, which are held horizontally to the small pouch and dorsal petal.

Odontoglossums and their allied hybrids
Odontoglossums come from the New World and nearly all are high altitude plants from the Andes. Although they grow close to the equator there, they enjoy the cool, airy conditions of the cloud forest high in the mountains, where there is little difference between the seasons and the days remain the same length all the year round. This produces an ideal climate of permanent 'spring' where the days are never too hot or the nights too cold. From this idyllic region come the Odontoglossums which are the most popular among thousands of different orchids. The modern hybrids produced in cultivation far from their natural habitat acclimatise easily to a temperate climate, provided they are given plenty of fresh air to keep them cool in the summer and artificial heat during the winter. Because these conditions are not easily met in the home, they are not

22

very successful as house plants. However, when Odontoglossums are crossed with closely related genera, hybrids are produced with a vigour which makes them far more suitable for indoor growing.

Not all the Odontoglossums originate from South America: there is a large branch of this family which comes from north of the Panama Isthmus, including the region up through Guatemala to Mexico. Naturally, with such a wide distribution there is considerable variation in the habit of the plants and type of flowers they produce, although all require similar culture.

Odontoglossums are bulbous orchids, producing a new bulb each growing season. A flowering sized plant may consist of four or five bulbs with a new growth. As the young plant progresses to maturity, each bulb produced is larger and more vigorous than the previous one, but this is only achieved with correct culture! Each bulb may carry two or three leaves which will last for several years, the old bulbs shedding their leaves first. An average plant consisting of five bulbs will probably have two without leaf, the three younger bulbs carrying between six and ten leaves between them. As the new growth reaches maturity and develops its bulb, the flower spike will appear from the base. Depending upon the variety it may carry from two to three or up to a dozen or more flowers, often on a tall arching spray. The flowering period is mainly during the spring or autumn months.

Before discussing the best plants to grow and the hybrids within this genus it is important to look at two other related genera with which Odontoglossums will interbreed to produce much easier plants to grow.

Miltonias, particularly the soft leaved varieties, come from the same Andean rain forest as the Odontoglossums, where they also grow upon the trees as epiphytes. They have achieved a similar habit of growth although with smaller bulbs and much more foliage, which is a beautiful soft green. Their flamboyant blooms are large and rounded and extremely colourful, and Miltonias are often called the 'pansy orchid' owing to the large round shape of the flower which resembles this popular bedding plant.

Oncidiums are a much larger genus with a greater diversity of flower, colour, shape and size, and are widely distributed throughout the tropics of both North and South America. Their habit of growth and structure of bulbs more closely resembles the species among the Odontoglossums.

Among the Odontoglossum species there are still quite a number which are obtainable and suitable for growing indoors. Although becoming scarce in the wild they propagate readily in the commercial greenhouses, and in this way their stocks are maintained. *Odontoglossum grande* is a beautiful orchid which, with a couple of others, stands apart from the rest of the orchids in this genus. Originally from Guatemala, it produces dark green pseudo bulbs and thick broad leaves. The flowers, which appear in the autumn, are huge, up to 12 cm (5 in.) across, and highly glossed. Three to five can be produced on a stem. They are boldly coloured yellow, barred with rich chestnut, and in the centre of the flower

Odontoglossum grande. 'The clown orchid' has been popular indoors for many years and is certainly one of the best varieties to grow. Flowers are rich yellow and chestnut brown.

can be seen a form resembling the figure of a man, which gives this plant its common name 'clown orchid'. Unfortunately, this species has resisted just about all attempts to hybridise it, and there are few hybrids. Those which have been produced do not compare with the beauty of the species. The plant starts its new growth late in the spring after its winter rest and should be kept watered throughout the summer growing season. With the approach of autumn the bulb matures and the flower spike emerges. After flowering, the mature bulb goes into its rest for the winter. It is important to give this species a complete rest, keeping it in a dry state in full light. This winter treatment is essential to ensure flowering the

24

following year; if insufficient light is given during the winter, it will be unlikely to bloom. Being a very cool growing orchid it is best housed in a window where the light is good all the year round.

Other Odontoglossum species which may be tried as house plants include *O. bictoniense*, a soft, green leaved species from Mexico which is continuously growing and which produces long upright sprays of up to twenty-five pretty flowers. The petals are green barred with brown, the heart shaped lip is white often suffused with pink. Flowering during the summer, it will continue to bloom for many weeks. *O. pulchellum*, has pure white flowers with yellow centres which are produced from oval shaped bulbs which bear two narrow leaves. This species is fragrant and also comes from Mexico. It propagates and divides easily. None of the South American species of Odontoglossum or Miltonia are available these days as house plants. They will only be found in cultivation in limited quantities in botanical collections where they have become collector's items, or in the stud houses of orchid breeders.

Oncidium species which are readily available and recommended for indoor growing are *Oncidium tigrinum* from Mexico which has a habit of growth closely resembling that of the Odontoglossums, while the flowers are carried on long branched sprays. The most prominent feature of all Oncidiums is the lip, and that of *tigrinum* is no exception. This is large and rounded, and coloured a bright canary yellow. The petals are smaller, yellow patterned in dark brown, and on bright days when the atmosphere is right, it produces a strong perfume. *Oncidium ornithorynchum*, by contrast, produces short, branched sprays of numerous, densely clustered, rosy pink flowers with twisted and curled petals. This species is often grown solely for its beautiful fragrance. *Oncidium incurvum* has long, branched spikes of pale pink flowers with pink and white lips. Up to a hundred blooms are produced on a spray. *Oncidium tigrinum*, *ornithorynchum* and *incurvum* all come from Mexico where they are used to growing in a drier atmosphere than some of the jungle plants, making them more easily adaptable to culture indoors.

As already mentioned, the Odontoglossum species from South America are not to be recommended for indoors. However, the numerous hybrids from them are worth trying, particularly where they have been crossed with Miltonias to produce the genus *Odontonia*, or with Oncidiums to produce *Odontocidium*. The little known genus *Cochlioda*, which is seldom seen in cultivation today, produces bright red flowers and has been used extensively for breeding with Odontoglossums to produce the genus *Odontioda*. When an Odontioda is crossed with a Miltonia the result is

25

a trigeneric cross. This was first achieved by a Belgian grower, Mr Vuyl-steke, who gave this hybrid the new generic name of *Vuylstekeara*. Another example is *Wilsonara* which is the result of combining Odonto-glossum, Cochlioda and Oncidium. These complex hybrids are ex-tremely difficult to breed, but once they have been produced they are usually very easy to grow. Because of the different species represented in the one hybrid they are much stronger and more vigorous in cultivation and the flowers bear the best characteristics of shape and size from the

Odontocidium Crow-borough. *This is prob-ably the the most widely grown Oncidium hybrid and generally succeeds very well indoors. Very tall sprays are produced by mature plants.*

different parents. One of the most famous hybrids available today is *Vuyl-stekeara* Cambria 'Plush' FCC/RHS (First Class Certificate awarded by The Royal Horticultural Society, London). This outstanding plant, which was originally raised in the 1930s, has never been superseded and with modern methods of mass propagation is available for everyone to grow. It produces long sprays of deep, wine red flowers, with a large spreading white lip heavily peppered with red. Today this plant has become popular all over the world, and because of its complicated breeding it will adapt to growing in warm or cool conditions. *Odontocidium* Tiger Butter is a hybrid from *Oncidium tigrinum* in which the characteristics of that fine species have been enhanced to produce a rounded flower with a large yellow lip and broad glossy petals which far surpass the species flower. *Wilsonara* Widecombe Fair is, by contrast, a very open, star-shaped bloom which is a first generation hybrid from *Oncidium incurvum*. A large plant will produce a hundred flowers on a massive branched spike. These hybrids and many others are best grown in a cool room where the light is good but away from all direct sunshine. The same applies to the numerous and excellent Miltonia hybrids which are so readily available

Vuylstekeara Cambria 'Plush' FCC/RHS. *This world famous hybrid is one of the finest of its type. The petals and sepals are rich mauve/ red, while the lip is white heavily dotted with dark red.*

today, and are obtainable in reds, whites, yellows, plum colours as well as pinks and endless combinations of these shades.

The multigeneric hybrids are continuously growing plants. The only time they are not growing is when they are producing their flower spikes. Because the new growth follows immediately after the plant has finished flowering, these plants should be kept watered throughout the year. They can be allowed to dry out slightly during the winter months, but otherwise, the compost must be kept evenly moist to encourage a steady, continuous rate of growth. Among the species, those varieties which do not rest such as *Odontoglossum bictoniense*, should be watered as the hybrids,

27

while those which cease their growth during part or all of the winter should be allowed to dry out, although not to such an extent that their bulbs shrivel. Should this occur, give one very thorough watering and keep the plant slightly wetter until the bulbs regain their plumpness.

Cymbidiums

Cymbidiums, like so many orchids, are widely distributed in the wild. They occur in an area of the Far East which stretches from the Himalayas, China and the southern islands of Japan, through the East Indies to the northern territories of Australia. Most of the species are of botanical interest only, with small, insignificant flowers. Also among the Cymbidiums can be found an extraordinary species of minute plant which grows under the ground and produces small flowers on a short spike about 8 cm (3 in.) high. None of these more obscure species have qualities which make them worth using for breeding purposes.

A typical Cymbidium from which the bulk of hybrids have been raised produces egg shaped bulbs, completely covered by the leaves. These leaves are up to 1 m (3 ft) long and there are eight to ten per bulb. As is typical of orchids, Cymbidiums grow in enormous clumps in the wild, but in cultivation are maintained at a convenient size; a large plant will consist of eight to ten bulbs in a 30 cm (12 in.) pot. The hybrids have been produced mainly from species which grow at high altitudes in cool, airy forests either as terrestrials in the ground where the soil is well drained, or as epiphytes growing in the forks of large trees where there is space for them to expand into large clumps.

In cultivation the hybrids produce their flowering spikes from the base of the latest completed bulb during the late summer. These spikes grow continuously for six months or more before opening their blooms on long stems during the winter and spring months. The spikes may be 1 m (3 ft) long with anything up to twenty blooms, depending upon the variety, in a range of colours from the soft pastel shades of pink and white, yellow and green, to the rich reds and bronzes. The lip is white or cream and heavily or lightly coloured around the edge. This colouring varies from the most delicate spotting, to heavy, all over blotching, barred with crimson. The flowers are amongst the longest lasting of all orchids; eight to ten weeks in perfection is not unusual. They have become the most popular cut flower with the florist and the blooms can commonly be seen for sale in shop windows, usually as individual blooms in cellophane packs.

Cymbidiums are the largest of the cultivated orchids and can become very space consuming. For this reason they are not the most suitable for growing on a window sill or in a small room. Requiring space in which to grow and plenty of air and light, they are ideally suited to the garden room or sun lounge.

The Cymbidium hybrids can be divided into two types: the standard or largest varieties, and the miniatures which have been bred along different lines to produce a much smaller plant. These miniature Cymbidiums are better suited to the window sill and can be obtained in the same range of colours as the larger varieties. While in the standard

Cymbidium Buddah. This large, modern hybrid shows excellent quality and the wide, well shaped lip typifies the best type of hybrid. Cymbidiums are produced in a multitude of colours.

varieties the hybridiser has strived to produce a bigger bloom, the miniatures have been bred to retain the same qualities in a more compact shape and size. They have therefore become very successful plants with both the home grower and the small greenhouse owner.

Like so many of our orchids today the Cymbidium species have become scarce and should not be handled by the beginner. The hybrids are far more suitable for the home grower. As with all other orchids, new varieties are produced by crossing two selected parents. The seedlings produce a wider range of plants which will bear some resemblance to each parent, but, like children in a family, no two will be exactly alike. With the

29

introduction of mass propagation by meristem culture, the finest varieties have now been made readily available at reasonable prices. It is quite possible for small home growers to have top quality awarded plants among their collections.

Unlike Odontoglossums and Cattleyas, Cymbidiums have no closely related genera with which they can be interbred. Therefore all the hybrids available are produced from pure, one genus, lines of breeding.

Although the standard Cymbidium is still more widely grown than the miniature varieties, we will discuss the smaller type first because they require less space and can be grown more easily in the home. The miniature hybrids have been produced from a limited number of species which are small in stature and which will produce flowers from a plant in an easily accommodated pot. The first miniature Cymbidiums were produced some sixty to seventy years ago, but at that time created little interest. They were, in fact, in advance of their time and in the last twenty years their popularity has increased enormously. The earliest hybrids were produced by crossing the species *Cymbidium pumilum*. This delightful little plant produces flower spikes about 10–12 cm (4–5 in.) long, carrying somewhat insignificant blooms. Although it is not recommended for the hobbyist as it can be difficult to grow and is now scarce in the wild, when crossed with standard Cymbidiums, the result is an ideal, compact plant with flower spikes to match. One of the first *C. pumilum* hybrids to create much interest arose when *C. pumilum* was crossed with the standard Cymbidium species *C. lowianum*, giving some idea of what could be achieved. As a first generation primary the flowers were plentiful but star-shaped, with narrow petals and sepals. This hybrid is called *C.* Pumilow. Later, when *C. pumilum* was crossed with the large modern hybrids, far better results were achieved and well rounded flowers were produced in an almost endless range of colours. Once second generation crossings began to appear, even more improvement was made. Today the best of these hybrids are represented by the famous line of Showgirls, which are available in a multitude of pastel colours, mainly pink and white.

The second most important miniature Cymbidium used in hybridising is *C. devonianum*. This plant has virtually no pseudo bulbs and produces wide, dark green foliage, and a pendant flower spike with numerous flowers. These are olive green in their colouring, the sepals and petals are overlaid with dark red lining and the lip is purple. This plant has given rise to many beautiful hybrids mostly of dark rich colouring such as *C.* Touchstone 'Mahogany' which is a deep brown red. Other well known varieties are *C.* Goblin which is green and *C.* Bulbarrow

Cymbidium Putana. *Flowers of delicate, pastel shades are produced by this compact hybrid which has been raised from the species* C. pumilum.

Cymbidium Goblin. *Miniatures such as this are more easily accommodated indoors than the standards and can be every bit as attractive. This hybrid has been raised from the species* C. devonianum.

31

which has similar colouring to the parent species with solid coloured lips.

From these two species, *C. pumilum* and *C. devonianum*, have arisen two completely different hybrid lines. The *C. pumilum* hybrids are recognisable by their clear pastel shades and delicately spotted lips, while, in complete contrast, the hybrids from *C. devonianum* are richly coloured, in reds and greens. The solid crimson colouring of the lips in *devonianum* hybrids makes these miniatures quite unique among Cymbidiums, for this feature is not found in the standards to the same extent. The beauty of the miniatures is that they can be contained in as little as a 15 cm (6 in.) pot, they are easily handled and do not present the problems which occur with handling massive standard Cymbidiums. However, if allowed to grow on for several years without being divided, they can make very large specimen plants. Otherwise they can be kept small by dividing and removing back bulbs. Of course, the larger the plant, the more spikes produced in a season, resulting in a far better show of flowers. The *C. pumilum* hybrids produce upright spikes, while those bred from *devonianum* retain the pendant form, and will give a beautifully cascading or arching spray. Alternatively, if preferred, they can be trained in an upright position where sufficient headroom is available; it is a matter of personal choice.

In contrast to the above plants the standard Cymbidium has been produced from a handful of species of the most decorative type. Here the hybridiser has continually strived to produce larger and rounder flowers in a wide range of colours and varieties. The best of these produce long, many flowered spikes over 1 m (3 ft) high and are the result of many generations of interbreeding which has continued for decades. The hybrids seen today bear no resemblance to the species from which they originated. If one has the room in which to grow these plants, preferably a sun lounge, then these highly decorative orchids will produce a beautiful display in the winter and early spring. At this time of the year when there are few flowers to grace the room, they are most welcome.

Some of the most popular varieties are *C.* Balkis and its related hybrids which produce perfectly round flowers in colours ranging from pure white, through many shades of cream and yellow to the pastel pinks which contain Vieux Rose in their parentage and are well known for their spotted lips, to the dark pinks and reds famous for their rich colourings. In contrast to these are the vibrant greens of Nicky, Fort George and Miretta which steal the stage with their red or spotted lips. Another exciting colour is yellow, which ranges from pale primrose to the golden yellow of Cariga and the pre-Christmas Angelica. With the exception of blue and its near shades, any colour can be found, and the beginner or novice grower may do better asking for a plant by colour rather than quoting a particular name to the nurseryman. With new hybrids arriving on the market so fast, some names can quickly become outdated. For complete satisfaction it is better to ask the nurseryman for a green Cymbidium with a red lip and leave the choice of variety to him.

Cymbidium Ann Green. *Excellent, large modern hybrids such as this produce a wonderful display but are only suitable for a large room or sun lounge. The blooms will last for many weeks during the spring months.*

Cymbidiums grow all the year round merely slowing the rate of their growth during the winter in accordance with the shorter days and lower temperatures. With their extensive root system they can absorb large quantities of water and this should not be restricted during the spring and summer when their growth is at its maximum. The watering should be reduced slightly during the winter to keep the plants just evenly moist without allowing them to dry out completely. They will also benefit from regular overhead spraying throughout the summer with application of liquid feed every ten days or so.

33

Cattleyas and their allied hybrids

Cattleyas are tropical orchids which originate from the jungles of Central and South America. Their distribution covers an area from Mexico in the north, through Guatemala, Colombia, Ecuador to Peru in the south, and the forests of Venezuela and Brazil. Many of the most important and showy flowers come from the last two countries. Their habit of growth is unusual and their bulbs are quite unlike any other orchid, being long and club shaped with the narrow part at the base. Each bulb carries either one or two thick leathery leaves and in the wild, the plants are found growing in enormous clumps consisting of hundreds of bulbs, each of which live for many years. These great masses grow epiphytically, high on the branches of the host trees, and they can be in danger of crashing to the ground should the branch break under the huge weight. In cultivation these plants more usually consist of five to eight bulbs per plant, at which size they are easily manageable. The bulbs are joined to each other by a thick woody rhizome which sits on top of the compost and is clearly visible as part of the plant, unlike other orchids where the rhizome is underground and unnoticed. The flowering sheaths are produced from the apex of the completed bulb, and it is from these sheaths that the flower buds emerge, generally during the spring or autumn months. The sheath protects the buds at the earliest stage of their development until they literally burst out and open within a few days. Generally two or three enormous blooms are produced from a single bulb. These wonderfully flamboyant flowers are among the largest of the cultivated orchids.

The Cattleya species fall into two distinct groups: plants with one leaf per bulb are unifoliates, and plants with two leaves of equal size on each bulb are of the bifoliate type. Although the flowering habits of the two types are similar, the unifoliates produce much larger, more showy flowers. The bifoliates are noted for producing many more blooms per stem, which, although smaller in size, lack none of the exotic beauty of their larger cousins and are often more richly coloured. The unifoliate flowers come in colours ranging from white through lavender to deep mauve with a few yellow strains, and the bifoliates range from white through pink to deep copper shades with yellow and green incorporated. The colour ranges have become intermingled through hybridisation and have been greatly extended by further breeding with a number of closely related genera.

As with the Odontoglossums, a number of new man-made genera have been developed which incorporate the qualities of the originals. The Catt-

34

leya species are also in the same position as the South American Odonto-glossums and their allies, with very few found in cultivation today because the plants have become scarce in the wild and are no longer imported on a regular basis. However, for the purpose of the indoor grower, the hybrids are far more showy and rewarding to grow anyway, being more tolerant and easily catered for.

Closely related and similar in appearance to the Cattleyas are the Laelias. This genus comes from the same parts of the world as the Cattleyas and is very variable in habit and appearance. It is the Brazilian varieties which have become the most important of their genus in hybridisation with Cattleyas. This cross produces the genus *Laeliocatt-leya* and combines the qualities of the two genera.

While it is true to say that the hybrids within this group provide extremely robust plants which have a wide tolerance making them most suitable for indoor growing, there are, nevertheless, two Laelia species which are worth growing. *Laelia anceps* and *L. gouldiana* both originate from Mexico where they are accustomed to a dry and sunny climate. Their blooms are carried on tall stems with up to four or five flowers being produced at the top. *L. gouldiana* produces a cylindrical bulb with two pointed leaves at the apex, from between which grows a flower spike about 50 cm (18 in.) long. The flowers are a rich rosy purple with a deeper purple lip. This plant has been a favourite with orchid lovers since early times and blooms regularly in the autumn. *L. anceps* has a similar habit of growth, but produces a single leaf from a more club shaped bulb. Its flowers are slightly smaller and are coloured a soft delicate shade of rosy pink. The lip is marked with deep mauve.

Another important genus closely related to the Cattleyas is the very small and compact Brazilian Sophronitis with its deep red flowers. While the Cattleyas and Laelias number many species in their groups, the Sophronitis is an extremely small genus with less than half a dozen species. Of these, *Sophronitis cernua* and *S. rosea* are collectors' items which belong in the greenhouse of the more experienced grower. Owing to their small stature and careful watering requirements they are not suited to indoor growing where the drier atmosphere is not conducive to their good health. The most noteworthy of this small genus is *S. coccinea*. The whole plant barely exceeds 5 cm (2 in.) in height and consists of small, slender or roundish bulbs topped with a single leaf. The flowers are produced usually singly, or occasionally two on a short stem from the apex of the bulb. Their flowering time is various and depends upon completion of the bulb. Unlike the Cattleyas and a number of the Laelias, the Sophronitis do not produce flowering sheaths; the buds emerge directly from the bulb.

While this beautiful little species is widely grown in cool greenhouse collections for its own undeniable beauty, its hybrids have added much to its related genera. *S. coccinea* has been crossed with Cattleyas to produce the genus *Sophrocattleya*, and with Laelias to produce *Sophrolaelia*, while a further step forward incorporates all three genera in *Sophrolaeliocattleya*. While these are the most well known genera incorporating

Laelia gouldiana. A highly coloured favourite for a cool room with a sunny position. The rich mauve blooms appear in the autumn and winter months.

Sophronitis, they are by no means all that is available. The main influence of the Sophronitis in these crosses has been to reduce the plant to a far more compact and manageable size, easily accommodated on the window sill, and to add the brilliant red colouring found in the species. While most of the hybrids produce smaller flowers, they are often produced in an abundance, while their brilliant colour outshines all other hybrids within this group. Although the majority of hybrids containing Sophronitis produce a multitude of red shades, other colours have come through, with orange and yellow being represented where different breeding lines have been used.

There is a further important genus which has also contributed greatly to the multigeneric hybrids within this group, and, as with the Sophronitis, it is mainly one single species which has been used for its breeding value. The genus *Brassavola*, which has a similar natural distribution to the above mentioned genera, contains many beautiful species, most of which are coloured a very light green. Of these, one species in particular, *Brassavola digbyana* is outstanding in its flower and breeding qualities. *B. digbyana* is now correctly known as *Rhyncolaelia digbyana*, but for registration purposes involving hybrids the older name has been retained to avoid confusion. The habit of this species is similar to the related genera, although the plant is slightly smaller in stature than the Cattleyas, the bulbs are slender and carry a solitary thick leaf, and the whole plant has a blue green colour. The species is considered to be very free flowering in sunny parts of the world, but in Britain it is often shy flowering due to the lack of sufficient light for part of the year. It is best suited to a sunny greenhouse and is not recommended for indoor growing for this reason. It may also soon become difficult to import. A single large bloom is produced which opens to the most delicate green without trace of another colour. The most outstanding feature of the flower is the very large, rounded and deeply frilled lip. This frill is found in no other species within this sub-tribe, and seldom met with in orchids at all. Its purpose is not immediately apparent, although it obviously has a function. While there are very few hybrids within this genus, there are a multitude of hybrids with the aforementioned Cattleyas etc. To these hybrids the Brassavola has added size, and shape of the lip, and, where it has been most predominant, some beautiful pastel shades. Unfortunately, the deep fimbriation of the lip has never been reproduced in any of the hybrids to the same degree. It is this species that has produced the Brassocattleyas etc.

In addition to those already mentioned, there are a number of other genera within the same sub-tribe which will interbreed with each other and which produce even more complex hybrids. These are not so widely grown, nor so easily cultivated, and are therefore only mentioned in passing.

When purchasing a Cattleya hybrid it may be more satisfactory to ask for the specific colour you require unless you are reading from a catalogue, so numerous are the hybrids. From the pure bred Cattleyas the colour choice is mainly mauves with perfectly shaped flowers as large as a plate. The best white hybrids such as have been produced along the Bow Bells line of breeding give a perfectly balanced flower of the purest white with yellow in the centre. Where the Brazilian Cattleyas and Laelias have been intercrossed, some of the most striking results have been large yellow flowers with purple or magenta lips sometimes deeply veined in the throat with a rich gold. When the small, bright red flowers of *Sophronitis coccinea* are mixed with the blood of Laelias and Cattleyas the result is some of the most vivid colours to be found in the orchid family. One of the most popular and easy to grow among these hybrids is *Sophrolaeliocattleya* Jewel Box. It blooms regularly and never becomes too large. As with Odontoglossums and Cymbidiums, this group of orchids is easily mass produced by meristem culture and excellent named varieties are readily available. With so much interbreeding it has become difficult to generalise on the size of these hybrids as they can vary considerably. As a guide, the pure Cattleya and mixed Brassolaeliocattleya hybrids will require 10–30 cm (8–10 in.) pots when mature, whereas those hybrids with Sophronitis or Laelia in their make-up are smaller and more compact.

So successful have these hybrids proved to be as house plants, they are now widely grown throughout the world. They are quite happy in warm conditions, especially the slightly drier atmosphere prevalent within the house. However, they can grow too large for the narrow window sill and would be better suited to the sun lounge which will enable them to receive all the light they require to bloom well.

The multigeneric hybrids within this group nearly all rest for several months at a time. This resting period varies and may not always coincide with winter but commences when the plant has completed one bulb, and finishes when that bulb has flowered. While growing, the Cattleya hybrids can be given considerable applications of water and regular feeding to maintain their fast rate of growth. Both should be lessened as the bulb nears completion and discontinued when development is complete and flowering imminent. After flowering, the new growth should be watched for, and when seen to be appearing from the base of the plant, normal watering can be resumed.

Phalaenopsis

Phalaenopsis are extremely beautiful orchids, with species to be found in India, down through Borneo and Malaysia to New Guinea, with the largest concentrations in the Philippines. They grow mainly in the steamy lowland forests where there is a constant moist atmosphere and very little direct sunlight. The plants grow upon host trees as epiphytes and often grow downwards.

Phalaenopsis do not produce pseudo bulbs but their leaves are extremely thick and fleshy and grow from the base of the plant. Usually one or two new leaves are produced from the centre of the plant in a season. An average sized plant in cultivation may have between three and six leaves at any one time and in some species they can grow to over 1 m (3 ft) in length. They may be plain dark green, or beautifully mottled and barred in silvery grey. The roots of the Phalaenopsis are the most attractive of any orchids; in the wild they attach themselves firmly to the bark of their tree, and run along its surface for some distance. These very fleshy roots are flat, silvery grey with a green or purple growing tip. In cultivation they will adhere to anything with which they come into contact. The flower spikes appear from the base of one of the younger leaves and can carry from just a few, to many, well rounded flat blooms.

Unlike so many orchids, the Phalaenopsis hybrids do not have a definite flowering season; owing to the various species in their make-up they tend to bloom at any time of the year and will last for many weeks in perfection. A large mature plant will often produce a new flower spike before the old one has finished flowering, with the result that a single plant can remain in bloom for many months. A further desirable feature of the Phalaenopsis is that the flower spike, when it has finished blooming, will produce further side shoots which in turn will have more flowers. It is not unusual for young plants to be produced in the same way from the tip of the side shoots on the old flower spike, and it is this that is used in propagation. While many of the species do this quite freely on a regular basis, most of the hybrids are more reluctant to produce offspring in this way, although it does occasionally happen. The colours of the Phalaenopsis, although restricted basically to pink and white with a little yellow, come in a variety of shades with different markings.

The Phalaenopsis are related to a number of different orchids, including Vandas, Renantheras and Doritis with which they will interbreed to produce intergeneric hybrids. However, these crossings greatly alter the growing requirements of the hybrid, which can become more demanding in its requirements for light. Generally speaking, for the home orchid grower, the pure bred Phalaenopsis are far more easily accommodated than the bigeneric hybrids, unless there is a very sunny position available. The pure bred Phalaenopsis hybrids are also often more free flowering.

Many of the Phalaenopsis species, especially those from the Malaysian Peninsula, are becoming scarce in cultivation as they dwindle in the wild. The species which are still common are mostly those from the Philippines, such as *Phalaenopsis amabilis, sanderana, stuartiana* and *schillerana*. These delightful, free flowering species have formed the basis for the majority of the modern hybrids. From *P. sanderana* and *P. schillerana* have come the pink coloured varieties, while *P. amabilis* has produced all the large, modern white varieties and *P. stuartiana* has added the attractive spotting of the lower petals and a variety of delightful lip markings.

Other hybrid types are being created by crossing these modern round hybrids with the smaller flowered species, such as *P. lueddmanniana* to give a further range of novelty types. These novelties often produce a

Phalaenopsis equestris. A delightful miniature species for a warm room. The long lasting blooms are white to pale pink, with a darker mauve/red lip.

much smaller plant with a short spray of compact flowers, which can be accommodated in a much smaller space.

Phalaenopsis are warm growing orchids which cannot stand the cooler temperatures of many of their counterparts. They would not be very happy standing on the kitchen window sill at room temperature unless it remained very warm during the day and night. Ideally their minimum night temperature should never drop to below 18°C (65°F) and they are even happier with a minimum of 21°C (70°F). The ideal place for growing Phalaenopsis is an indoor growing case, where the temperature can be controlled and kept up to their minimum requirements. They also make

40

very good subjects for the growing case because they do not require very much light to grow and flower well, and the artificial light suits them well. A number of the hybrids produce very long flower spikes when they are mature, and this should be borne in mind when placing them in the case. Their aerial roots will quickly adhere to the back or sides of the case, and this makes it difficult to move them once they have been positioned, without causing unnecessary damage. Another advantage of growing Phalaenopsis in the confines of a case is that the humidity can

Phalaenopsis Redfan. Large, well rounded white flowers with a contrasting red lip are produced by this hybrid on graceful sprays which can be produced at almost any time.

be kept that bit higher than for the other orchids growing outside, in the room.

The compost in which Phalaenopsis are grown should always be kept moist; the plants must not be allowed to become over wet at any time, nor completely dry for any period. More often than not their long fleshy roots will extend over the rim of the pot to seek moisture wherever they can find it, which may include the bottom of the water filled humidity tray. These roots should be allowed to meander and are often more healthy than those made inside the pot. The plants can be given additional liquid feed throughout the year where artificial daylight is available to

41

them. Spraying should be done in moderation only, too much water on the surface of the leaves can cause spotting and, at worst, rotting at the centre of the plant.

For anyone who is considering growing Phalaenopsis for the first time, the hybrids would be the obvious choice. As so often happens with breeding, the best qualities of the species are carried forward and combined in the hybrid to produce a much more robust plant which is more resistant to neglect. There is a much wider choice of colour and size among the hybrids, and plants can be chosen to fit into the amount of space available, bearing in mind the amount of head room which can be given to the plants. Where a number of Phalaenopsis plants are grown together, it is possible to have blooms all the year round, although one would need at least a dozen plants to achieve this perpetual display.

Phalaenopsis are also in great demand in many parts of the world for their cut flowers which are held in high regard by florists. In Europe especially, they are extensively cultivated for this market. Usually pure white varieties are grown, which are then dyed whichever colour required, in the same way that carnations are dyed. Phalaenopsis would be grown even more extensively by the amateur orchid grower if it were not for the fact that their high temperature requirements make them very expensive to cultivate in greenhouses. The home grower can grow them much more cheaply in an indoor case.

Dendrobiums

Dendrobiums are a tremendous genus of orchids both in numbers and beauty of their flowers. Very many species cover a large area of the world, spreading from Japan and parts of China, throughout India, the Malaysian Peninsula to New Guinea and Northern Australia. The majority of the species are sun loving and need a high humidity. This means that they are not ideally suited to indoor culture in general, but a few, mainly cool growing types found in India which have a dry resting period, can be successfully cultivated indoors where a sunny spot can be found for them.

The numerous species all produce tall, jointed stems which are elongated pseudo bulbs often referred to, for convenience, as canes. Those with tall canes produce leaves along their length, while other varieties which make shorter, club shaped bulbs produce leaves from the top portions only. Some of the varieties are evergreen while others have a deciduous rest and flower profusely along the length of the leafless cane. All the species regularly seen in cultivation are beautiful and many are fragrant.

Dendrobiums grow as epiphytes, the majority of them high in the forests where there is an abundance of moisture during the growing season followed by a dry period during which the orchids rest. Most of them produce an abundant, fine rooting system which often forms dense mats around the base of the plant. This holds them firmly in place on the tree branches and at the same time traps debris in the form of dead leaves which rot down to provide a meagre food supply for the plants. Most of the long caned varieties grow in a pendant position, their elongated bulbs being too heavy to support in an upright position, where they develop into huge clumps. Because they grow in the topmost parts and branches of the trees, they usually went unnoticed by the earlier travellers passing below, even when in full bloom. Often it was only their overpowering fragrance which attracted the collectors, who would then think nothing of chopping down the tree to obtain the specimens.

The breeding of hybrids from the Dendrobiums has not been carried out on such a gigantic scale as, for instance, with the Cymbidiums or Odontoglossums. The Dendrobiums have other genera with which they are related but none of these have been interbred. In the early days of orchid hybridisation many crosses were made between the various Dendrobium species, and a number of superb hybrids were produced. However, long lines of breeding were not developed as happened with the Odontoglossums and their allies in particular. Many of the hybrids raised using one well known species, *Dendrobium nobile*, were so similar in appearance that interest faded in the hybrid and the species remained popular. Other Dendrobiums produced nothing, or very little, of note and after a few hybrids these lines were dropped. However, after the turn of the century some very fine hybrids were produced from *D. nobile*, which even today cannot be surpassed. These *nobile* type hybrids, as they have become known, can grow exceedingly tall, over 1 m (3 ft) in height, and have lush, plump canes. They require a great deal of sunshine and light before they will display their blooms and large quantities of water at the roots while they are growing. A high humidity with regular overhead spraying is also beneficial, a requirement which generally makes them unsuitable for growing indoors, unless a sun lounge is available.

The following species are recommended only if a suitable sunny position can be found for them. Without sufficient light and full sunlight during the winter to ripen their canes, they will not bloom the following spring.

Rosy mauve is one of the most predominant colours to be found among the Dendrobiums, and many species are coloured in pastel or rich hues.

D. nobile sheds only part of its foliage under cultivation and will bloom during the spring months on canes which have retained their foliage. Flowered to perfection, two-thirds of the cane should be covered in bloom; flowers appearing in twos and threes from the sides of the bulb opposite the leaves. Growing indoors, fewer flowers are generally produced, but nevertheless they are extremely attractive. The sepals and petals are white, the rosy mauve colouring not quite covering the whole

Dendrobium nobile. An extremely popular orchid requiring a sunny position where its tall canes can ripen. Clusters of rosy mauve flowers with dark maroon centres are produced in the spring.

surface, and deepening towards the edge of the petals. The lip carries a deep maroon blotch. This species also has an albino variety, *D. nobile* var. *virginale* which, although it was very rare at one time, is happily now more easily available as nursery raised seedlings have replaced imported plants. This pure white form carries none of the rosy colouring, and the lip is a pale creamy yellow.

White is a colour frequently found in this genus. Many of the white flowered varieties have extremely large flowers, the largest in the genus. One particular favourite of note is *D. infundibulum*, in which the canes, young growths and sheaths on the flower buds are covered in small black

44

1 *Pleione formosana*. A delightful and hardy orchid. Following a winter resting period, new growth starts in early spring and is followed by flowers.

2 *Cymbidium* Bautista de Anza 'La Tuilerie'. Standard Cymbidiums will produce a wonderful display given sufficient room and light. They are winter and spring flowering in a wide variety of colours.

3 *Paphiopedilum insigne* 'Harefield Hall'. A very popular orchid which grows best in a cool, shady position. Various forms of this variety are available.

4 *Miltonia* Storm 'La Tuilerie'. Modern Miltonia hybrids do well in warm, shady and draught free places. The colour range extends from white to red, including pink and yellow.

5 *Laeliocattleya* Dusky Maid 'Christina'. This is one of many colourful Cattleya hybrids. It needs warmth and light to grow and flower indoors.

6 *Phalaenopsis* Rapture (left) and Redlip (right). Two beautiful orchids which should be kept away from direct sunlight but in a warm room. They bloom at any time of year and the flowers last many weeks.

7 *Odontoglossum rossii*. One of the most popular miniature Odontoglossums. It flowers mainly during winter and spring months and should be kept moist at all times.

8 Cool growing orchids which need plenty of light make an attractive window
display. The gravel filled trays contain water to give a humid microclimate.
On cold winter nights the plants should be moved away from the glass.

9 Orchids needing low light can be grown away from the window sill. They should never be placed on the television set, which produces a stream of warm, dry air.

10 An indoor case, used to house orchids permanently, can be made a beautiful feature of any room. The shade loving orchids will grow best in the artificial light.

11 A solid ball of white, healthy roots is a sign of a well grown and vigorous orchid. This Cymbidium is now potbound and needs repotting, or possibly 'dropping on'.

12 Sections of Dendrobium canes laid on moss or compost and kept moist and warm will grow to produce new plants. The transparent film is removed when the new growths start.

hairs. The canes carry dark green leaves along their length, which are shed in the autumn. In the spring the older canes produce crystalline white flowers from the top portion. These appear in twos and threes and are up to 10 cm (4 in.) across, each carrying a deep yellow stain in the throat. Another pretty species with similar foliage but on a smaller plant is *D. williamsonii*, which produces clusters of ivory white flowers on top of stoutish bulbs in the early summer. The lip is brightly coloured with a brick red stain, and it carries a lovely fragrance.

Dendrobium fimbriatum var. *oculatum. A tall, cool growing species which produces bright, golden yellow flowers in the spring following a winter rest. Note the delicate fimbriation around the edge of the lip.*

Species with flowers of the richest golden yellow are becoming increasingly difficult to obtain. *D. fimbriatum* var. *oculatum* is one of the showiest of this type. The tall, slender canes discard most of their foliage for the winter, and the older canes bloom over several years. The flowers are produced in the spring or early summer from a single truss, with up to eight or ten blooms. The deep golden yellow of the sepals and petals is set off against the deep maroon blotch in the beautifully fimbriated lip. Most of the yellow flowering varieties do not last in bloom for as long as many of the other coloured types.

45

The Dendrobiums mentioned here are the cool growing varieties from India; other varieties requiring heat can be tried, but they are by no means as easy indoors as the cooler growing types.

The watering of these orchids must be given careful attention if they are to bloom successfully. It is important that the plants receive as much water as possible from when the new growths commence until the bulbs have matured. Thereafter, they can be allowed to become completely dry for the duration of the winter, watering occasionally if undue shrivelling of the canes is noticed. During this time they must be given full light to ripen the newly completed bulbs. With *D. nobile*, watering should not be started until the plant is in advanced bud, otherwise the embryo buds are likely to turn into young plants. Feeding should be restricted to the growing season during which time rapid growth is made prior to the extended resting period.

We have stated the reasons why an orchid collection indoors should consist of mainly hybrids rather than the wild species of the world. There are, nevertheless, a few species which we feel sure will always remain with us. While they may become rare in the wild in the foreseeable future, they are among the most attractive and easily grown, and, because they are easily propagated in cultivation, their stocks will always remain in a number of orchid nurseries where demand for them by amateur growers will ensure that their numbers are never reduced. These few species can safely be recommended for indoor growing. All the following varieties are epiphytes requiring nothing special in the way of culture and can be mixed in with the Cymbidiums or Odontoglossums in a cool room.

Coelogynes

Coelogynes are a large genus of orchids, of which only a very few species are obtainable and desirable for indoor culture. The main colour to be found among these plants is white, but there is such a variety in size of flowers and lip markings that the following recommended varieties could all be grown without duplicating the same features.

Coelogynes are widely distributed in the wild, with the majority of the cultivated species coming from India. The plants grow as epiphytes and thrive in massive clumps, some several feet across, consisting of up to a hundred bulbs. The plants vary in size depending upon the species, but all produce handsome plants, with highly polished pseudo bulbs topped by a pair of dark green leaves. Some varieties produce an abundance of roots while others seem to make do with just a few spindly roots, just sufficient to hold their anchorage on a tree. Most of the species have a growing season followed by a resting period, during which time in cultivation they are left completely dry. The flowers appear from the apex of the leading bulb in some species, or from inside the new growth while it is still very young. More rarely, they are produced from the base of the previously completed bulb. A few varieties produce a flower spike which will bloom in successive years; when one season's blooms have finished, the stem remains green until the following year when more buds appear from the continuously growing tip. None of these species produces branched spikes, and few of them are very tall.

Only the species are grown to any extent in collections; the few hybrids which have been produced over the years are very rare and sought after. The easiest varieties to grow in the house are among the species. They are recommended for their ease of culture, which if correctly adhered to will reward the grower with a dazzling display of blooms in the spring. The following species are neat and compact growers, and can be easily accommodated on a window sill or wherever there is limited space available. However, it must be remembered that these species require winter light if they are to bloom successfully the following spring.

Coelogyne ochracea is the most delightful of orchids and appears to have everything for the home grower. The plant is neat and compact; it can be grown in an 8 cm (3 in.) container, and stands about 23 cm (9 in.) high in its pot. When the plant has completed its resting period, the new growth commences in the early part of the new year. The flower spikes appear from inside the new growth while it is still quite young and up to a dozen small, delightfully fragrant flowers are produced in the spring. These are a pure crystalline white, with the lip prettily marked in yellow and orange, and will last for about three weeks. Several new growths are usually produced in one season so several flowering spikes can be expected. Within a few years the plant will have doubled its size, and can be retained as a specimen, never becoming too large to be easily handled, or can be divided to retain the small pot size, according to the space available.

A similar and equally desirable species is *C. corymbosa*. This plant is slightly smaller than *C. ochracea*, and the bulbs a little rounder. The flowers appear slightly earlier in the spring, and last a good three weeks. Again, it is a species which readily produces several new growths each year and can grow quite large, but can easily be divided. The flowers are larger than *C. ochracea* with fewer carried on the sprays, which appear from the inside of the new growths. The blooms are the same crystalline

47

white, but the lip is beautifully patterned with orange and brown markings. This handsome little plant can be covered in blooms when grown to perfection. It lacks the sweet fragrance of *C. ochracea*.

A further white species is *C. cristata*, which has been recommended for indoor growing since the earliest days of orchid cultivation. Enormous plants are sometimes seen, which have been grown on window sills for many years and appear to be totally neglected; often growing in small

Coelogyne ochracea. A delightful miniature producing sparkling white flowers with orange and yellow markings on the lip. Spring blooming and fragrant.

pots so crammed with bulbs that new ones have to be produced on top of the older ones. However, it is in this state that the plant thrives, and provided it is given all the light it requires, even to the extent of placing it out of doors during the summer months, it will reward the grower with a mass of showy white flowers in the spring. These blooms appear on short flowering stems which grow from the base of the previous season's bulb. *C. cristata* is the largest flowered of the recommended species, and the only colouring is the deep yellow stain in the throat. It is an extremely beautiful species, often called 'the rag orchid', a term which apparently

48

refers to the ragged appearance of the petals which curl and crinkle, breaking up their outline.

While many other Coelogynes are available, the above species are those which will succeed best in an indoor environment, coping better than others with the drier atmosphere. Some varieties can become extremely large, particularly the warmer growing species which are not recommended. These are space consuming and require much light for most of the year. As their blooms are short lived, they give a poor return for the space they occupy in the home.

Coelogyne cristata. An all-time favourite for indoor growing. The large, glistening white flowers with deep yellow in the throat of the lip bloom throughout the winter and spring. Winter rest is important.

The watering requirements for Coelogynes are similar to those for Dendrobiums. The plants should be amply watered throughout the spring and summer while they are in active growth, to ensure the completion of good sized bulbs. During this time they can be lightly fed, and overhead sprayed if possible. During the winter they enjoy a complete rest and should remain as dry as possible, avoiding too much shrivelling of their bulbs, although a little shrivelling is a good thing and will improve their flowering performance the following spring.

Watering should commence as soon as the new growths are seen to be moving, this is particularly important with *C. ochracea*. If this species is kept too dry while in young growth, the leaves may become covered with a sticky substance which, if not washed off, can impede the development of the young growth and flower spike inside it. A curious feature occurs with *C. cristata* when the buds are near to opening. At this stage they turn brownish with a shrivelled, unhealthy look which can cause concern to the grower. This appearance is natural and within a couple of days the buds will open to reveal the full beauty of the blooms.

Encyclias

Among the Encyclias are a number of extremely attractive species. The following species were, until recently, known as Epidendrums, under which name they can be found in older books on the subject. *Encyclia cochleata* comes from Mexico, Guatemala and Honduras. The bulbs are curiously shaped, with a narrow base swelling out into a club shaped bulb which carries a pair of broad, light green leaves. The flowering spike appears from in between these leaves in the spring, and a green sheath protects its early development. The spike can be any length, depending upon the size and strength of the plant. A very young plant will produce a couple of flowers on a short spike, while a large specimen will produce up to a hundred flowers, on a flower spike which may be up to 1 m (3 ft) tall. These flowers will not all open at once, but will be produced over many months in a steady succession of bloom. It is not unusual for a large plant to continue in bloom for over a year, by which time the next bulb has been completed and is flowering in turn, so the plant becomes perpetually blooming. The individual flowers are green and black and the narrow petals and sepals form twisted green ribbons. The rounded lip, which gives rise to this plant's common name of 'cockleshell orchid', is very dark, almost black in colour and is placed at the top of the flower. It is an unusual feature among orchids for the lip to be held uppermost on the flower.

Another example of an 'upside down flower' is *E. pentotis.* In this species the pseudo bulbs are tall and slender and the two leaves are dark green. The two buds (occasionally only one) emerge from the sheath and open on a very short stem which barely exceeds the length of the sheath. The two flowers open back to back, resembling alighting butterflies. The colouring of the petals and sepals is a light creamy green, and the lip is streaked with red. Although these flowers only last from two to three weeks in the early summer, they are accompanied by the most delightful fragrance. This variety is one of a whole group of similar species all of which have a pale off-white colouring with a red lined lip, and are highly

50

fragrant. Most require similar culture, and some may be tried along with
E. pentotis.

A further interesting and showy species which does not resemble the
above two, is *E. vitellina.* This also comes from Mexico and Guatemala.
The bulbs are small and the leaves a dark blue green with a delicate bloom,
which is most apparent on the newly completed growths. The flower
spikes, which carry many flowers, can be up to 30 cm (1 ft) tall, and on
large plants they will branch once or twice. The star-shaped flowers are
vermillion red, sometimes varying to orange red, and the small neat lip
at the bottom of the flower is orange red. The main flowering season is
spread through the summer and autumn months. Because there are very
few red flowers among the orchids, this plant is especially desirable and
for its brightness, it is not easily surpassed. It likes to grow on the dry
side, which makes it ideal for indoors, and it should always be kept in
as small a pot as possible. The Encyclias are a very large and variable group
of orchids; we have recommended only three species which, while hardly
representative of the genus as a whole, do provide useful plants which
may be added to a collection.

The Encyclias recommended have a growing period followed by a resting period during which time they should be kept on the dry side, watering occasionally to prevent any shrivelling of the the bulbs. The plants
can be given liquid feed during the most active months of the year when
they should not be allowed to dry out. *E. vitellina* should be grown slightly
drier at all times than the other species and the leaves should not be sprayed
or wiped with water which would remove the protective bloom.

Lycastes

No section on indoor orchids would be complete without some mention
of the Lycastes. These are extremely attractive orchids of which one or
two of the more easily obtained species may be tried. There has been
a tremendous amount of work done on breeding the Lycastes and many
fine hybrids have been produced, including bigeneric hybrids of the man-
made genus *Angulocaste,* which are the result of crossing Lycastes with
Anguloas. These plants are superb growers but can become too large for
indoors as they produce extensive foliage and are very space consuming
when grown to perfection. The Lycaste species are smaller growers,
although even they require sufficient room for their spreading leaves during the summer months. Their bulbs are plump and hard, and are topped
by several large leaves which are paper thin and very easily damaged by
water droplets or rough handling. These leaves are usually shed before

51

the onset of winter and the plants remain in a dormant, leafless state until the new growth commences in the spring, often at the same time as the buds appear. When the leaves have turned yellow and are discarded naturally by the plant, spiteful thorny remains are left at the top of each bulb. No doubt this serves the plant as a protection in the wild, but they can give a painful scratch to the unwary!

Lycaste virginalis. Large, triangular white flowers with rosy pink flushing are enhanced by the darker coloured lip. Mainly winter flowering after which the foliage is shed.

The plants come from South America where they grow upon the rocks and trees in shady places. Under cultivation they do well in cool conditions similar to those preferred by the Cymbidiums. Their flowering season is mainly spring and early summer. The following varieties are the most easily obtained and are by no means rare due to the ease with which they propagate in cultivation. *Lycaste aromatica* and *L. cruenta* are two excellent varieties well worth looking out for; either or both may be tried although they differ slightly from each other. *L. aromatica* produces several flower buds from the base of the leading leafless bulb along with the new growth during the spring. The buds develop at a faster rate than the growth and the flowers have finished by the time the growth has reached the same height. Each stem carries a single, triangular shaped bloom which is a deep golden yellow colour and, as the name implies, is beautifully fragrant. *L. cruenta* produces similar flowers, but they are larger and lack the beautiful fragrance. Its flowers may be bolder than the former species and their colouring is yellowy green. A distinct species with unusual colouring is *L. deppei*. In this variety, which behaves as the two already mentioned, the flowers have pure white petals but for the lip which is yellow with a few red spots and the prominent sepals are green overlaid with brown speckling. A further lovely variety which blooms much earlier than the above is *L. virginalis*. The blooms are larger and produced on taller stems, often in the late autumn. The colouring is very variable and the flowers may be white shaded with pink, the lip white or pink shaded with red. It is altogether a delightful orchid and, unlike the foregoing, this species usually retains its foliage through the winter shedding it in the spring, before the commencement of the new growth.

With the start of new growth in the spring, the Lycastes proceed at a fast rate of growth and can be copiously watered throughout the spring and summer, together with liberal applications of liquid feed. By the end of the summer their bulbs should have been completed and as they mature their growth slows and stops altogether, a process observed by the yellowing and discarding of their foliage. From this time on they will need to be kept completely dry at the roots and placed in a position of full light to ripen their dormant bulbs. This ripening of the bulbs is an all important factor to their producing blooms the following spring. The buds usually show at the same time as the new growth, and watering must be done carefully at first to ensure that the buds do not become wet and that no water is allowed to lodge inside the new growth. Water must be kept from the foliage at all times to prevent ugly spotting and disfigurement.

Attractive miniatures
In addition to the orchids already recommended for indoor culture, we would like to draw our readers' attention to the following brief list of further species which can be grown with the assurance that they are not rare in the wild and that plants can be easily and quickly propagated in nurseries in this country. With their miniature size and pretty flowers they are ideal subjects where space is severely limited. However, they are by no means flamboyant, and in some cases can be said to be an

acquired taste. If you want something small and pretty, these are dainty miniature orchids of great charm.

Odontoglossum rossii, *cervantesii* and *stellatum* are three delightful miniature Odontoglossums which take up very little room and can be accommodated in 8 cm (3 in.) pots. The flowers are pretty and colourful and grow slightly higher than the foliage.

The Vandas are a large, beautiful group of orchids which usually enjoy high temperatures and maximum light all the year round, combined with a constantly high humidity. For these reasons they do not generally make good house plants, and are to be avoided. However, there is just one Vanda species which is quite unlike the rest. This is *Vanda cristata* which comes from India and produces a neat growing plant with pairs of slender leaves on an upright stem. The flowers, which are produced in abundance during the summer, are green, and the lip is white streaked with red. Provided a sunny window can be found *V. cristata* will be a most attractive addition to the miniature orchids.

Another unusual and attractive species from India is *Cirrhopetalum guttulatum*. This carries small bulbs along a creeping rhizome with a single leaf to each bulb. The small flowers appear in the summer and early autumn and are pale yellow spotted with purple. Placed as they are, side by side in a semi-circle, they produce a delightful effect on this free flowering plant.

It must be remembered that these miniature orchids growing in small pots will dry out quicker than those in larger pots, and their watering requirements should be checked more often. The miniature Odontoglossums produce small bulbs, and if allowed to become too dry at any time, they will quickly shrivel. During the winter these plants should be kept slightly drier than in the summer. This also applies to the Vanda and Cirrhopetalum, both of which require more winter light. The plants may be lightly fed during the summer months and the Vanda will enjoy regular spraying, especially if it is producing aerial roots. These miniatures are all cool growing and will be quite happy in a minimum temperature of between 10 and 12°C (50–55°F).

PART II

Caring for Orchids in the Home

For many years orchids were considered to be the elite of all greenhouse plants, requiring specially built glasshouses and carefully controlled conditions. This was certainly true in the earliest days of orchid cultivation when knowledge of them was limited and the plants obtained were those which had been imported from the wild. However, several decades of selective breeding have produced a wide variety of hybrids for the potential grower which not only produce larger and more colourful flowers, but will bloom more freely, and, most important of all, will grow happily in a variety of surroundings. These plants have an extremely wide tolerance with requirements which are simple and easy to reproduce almost anywhere. While there can be no doubt that the finest specimens will be achieved in greenhouse conditions where the light, temperature and humidity can be exactly balanced to satisfy their individual needs, the same plants will produce a brave show given similar conditions indoors, although their growth may be slower.

A greenhouse can produce ideal conditions for growth if properly managed at all times, but it can, if neglected for only a short period during adverse weather conditions, become a death trap for its occupants. Severe wintry weather with temperatures falling below freezing, or excessive mid-summer heat which is allowed to rise above 38°C (100°F), through inadequate shading or lack of ventilation, can result in the death of the plants. Less dramatic dangers await the plant growing indoors. Here the conditions in which *we* live comfortably are unlikely to allow the orchids to freeze to death or suffer intolerable heat.

Orchids are delightful and rewarding plants to cultivate and enthusiasts become extremely fond of the plants in their care. It is understandable, therefore, that many should want to grow their prized plants near at hand where they can be looked at and enjoyed to the full. One of the greatest faults with many greenhouses, is that they are erected at the very bottom of the garden, so that a long trek is needed to visit. This often means that visits to the orchids are put off for a few hours or even a few days because it is raining or it is not convenient. Some owners only visit their greenhouses at weekends, and this is simply not sufficient to keep healthy stocks of plants, whatever they may be. It is no wonder that these neglected objects fail to thrive as they should. How much better it is under these circumstances to bring the plants into the home where they can have attention lavished upon them.

Finding the right place
In the average modern home which is warm, light and airy there are many places where orchid plants can be grown. Conditions will vary from room to room and, depending upon their requirements, plants may be accommodated on a sunny window sill, or upstairs in a bathroom, which is poorly lit but well heated. There is also the kitchen which is usually far better lit and ventilated than many other rooms, being a working area of the house. All these places can be adapted to suit the needs of a particular plant. It is advisable to provide a number of suitable locations throughout the house for your orchids, so that plants can be moved around until the ideal spot is found for each one. The most important factor is not where a plant may *look* at its best, but where it will *grow* at its best. A bare, unlit corner of the living room may be crying out for decoration, but is not a suitable place in which to grow a plant. However, it can be used as a display area in which orchids may be placed while in bloom for a few weeks, later to be returned to their growing area. The needs of the plants must have precedence and it will be seen that a house can be divided into suitable growing and display areas. There are areas in any room which will be found to be quite unsuitable and must be avoided. These may include places where there is a direct draught of cold air for example. Warm draughts can also be harmful, such as hot air rising from a radiator or other source of heat.

In the older type of house or cottage where small windows let in limited light, different orchids should be attempted to those grown in the modern bungalow, house or flat. Here the larger picture windows and open plan design provide much more natural sunlight which will enable a much wider range of orchids to be grown.

Living room

Of all the rooms in the house, the best place to grow your orchids must surely be where you spend the greater part of your time—the living room. Here the whole family and friends can enjoy the sight of happy, flourishing orchids. With someone always close at hand, the plants will benefit from the constant attention to their needs, rather than being tucked away in a seldom visited part of the house. Where, in the living room, you decide to arrange your display must depend on the requirements of the plants. Orchids which like plenty of light and cool conditions will grow permanently on the window sill, while the more tropical varieties which like warmth but should never receive prolonged direct sunlight, will flourish on the coffee table or sideboard. A group of plants growing together in a bay window can look very attractive and form part of the decor of the living room. However, it must be remembered that unless double glazing is installed there will be a very cold area at night between the drawn curtains and the window. If the plants cannot be accommodated in a position on the inside of the curtains, they should be brought further into the room on cold winter nights. During the summer months the direct sunlight may be too bright for some plants and protection such as net curtains should be provided to prevent scorching of the foliage.

It is fashionable nowadays to stand plants and flowers on the television set. While this may look most attractive, nothing could be worse for the plant, which is subjected to a warm draught of air whenever the set is turned on. It is not always realised how much heat is given off by a television set. Gas or paraffin heaters are also dangerous to orchids, giving off fumes which may not be detectable or dangerous to human occupants but which can adversely affect the plants.

Bathroom

Many people, having found their sitting room an unsuitable growing area for some reason, turn to their bathroom in which to house their orchids. This can be successful if it is a large room where the natural light is filtered through frosted glass and therefore poor. It may be suitable for the shade loving tropical orchids which will cope with poor light and benefit from the humidity; many bathrooms incorporate an airing cupboard and are very warm. In the average bathroom suitable spaces for growing plants are limited as are the number of varieties which will succeed there.

Kitchen

The next most popular room in the house for growing plants is the kitchen. Since it is a working area in common use it is natural that the room should be at a comfortable temperature and the steam created by cooking provides a good supply of humidity. However where gas is installed for cooking, as with heating, there may be trouble from the fumes. Unfortunately, because it is a working area, space is often limited in the kitchen but a room divider in a combined kitchen/dining room can be turned into a real and interesting feature of the room with a little indoor gardening. Here orchids can be used successfully with other plants to great advantage.

Sun lounge

Home extensions and sun lounges are a feature of many houses today and these provide light airy places where many plants can thrive in near greenhouse conditions. Popular features of these home leisure areas are fish pools and fountains, providing humidity and ideal settings for the larger house plants such as rubber trees, palms, pineapples and oranges, making an all year round sub-tropical indoor garden. Here the largest of the orchids, which would be oversized in the living room, can be grown in tubs.

Cellar

Excellent results can also be obtained by growing orchids in cellars of old houses, which have been successfully converted into complete growing rooms for orchids. The advantage here is that the environment created is wholly artificial and controllable. Although the installation costs are high, running costs are extremely low, with virtually no loss of heat. The walls and ceiling are first covered with polystyrene for insulation, and then lined with tin foil which reflects maximum light into the room. The plants are grown on a bench lit by tubular lights using special bulbs designed for plant growth. These are operated by a time switch giving the equivalent of daylight hours required, but at night, thus using off-peak electricity with considerable saving. Very often the heat given off by these lights is sufficient to make additional forms of heating unnecessary. A manual switch enables the grower to inspect the plants at any time of the day. Although this method of cultivation is successful, it is somewhat specialised, and it is only possible to grow a limited variety of plants under these conditions. Basically, depending upon the minimum temperature which is maintained, the types will be limited to those warm, shade loving plants which cannot tolerate direct sunlight.

It is possible to purchase ready-made greenhouse benches which can be installed in your cellar, as the amount of head room available is usually about the same as in a greenhouse. Alternatively, you can construct your own benches quite easily, tailor-made to fit the space available. In a standard bench the top will probably consist of galvanised iron or fibreglass trays 5–8 cm (2–3 in.) deep, which can be filled with gravel and kept moist.

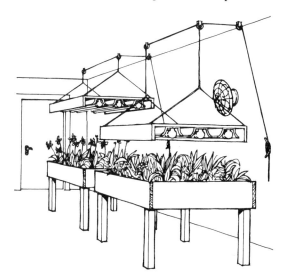

A typical set up for cellar cultivation. The plants stand on benches which incorporate deep, gravel filled trays to retain the excess water. The batteries of lights can be raised or lowered to accommodate plants both in and out of bloom. The fan maintains a continuous circulation of air inside the room and the door can be opened for extra ventilation.

The home-made version could consist of a shallow box lined with polythene. This type of bench is an essential part of cellar culture, as it is from here that the humidity will be created for the moist atmosphere so necessary for the health of the plants. The tray will collect the surplus water from watering and spraying of the plants and prevent spillage onto the floor.

The plants should be placed on upturned pots or saucers to avoid any direct contact with the water and the subsequent danger of them becoming overwatered or too wet at the roots. If the plants are of a uniform height, or made so by varying the height of the supporting pots, the tube lights can be made up into batteries attached to a wooden frame. These are suspended from the ceiling by pulleys so that the entire lighting system

59

can be raised to allow inspection of the plants for watering and general attendance, and lowered to the most suitable height above the plants enabling the maximum use to be made of the lights. While the lights should be as close to the plants as possible (the distance will be determined by the tallest flower spike), they should not be so close that the heat generated causes damage or scorch to any part of the foliage or buds.

Ventilation is important to orchids wherever they are grown, and must be amply provided in the cellar to ensure a continuous supply of fresh air. To maintain a degree of freshness and keep a movement of air, a small electric fan can be used to play air over the top of the plants. This will assist in keeping the air fresh and at the same time will dry up excess water from the foliage after watering. It will also prevent the plants from overheating through contact with the lights. If windows are available, they should be opened for a complete change of air whenever the outside temperature is not so cold as to cause a draught or sudden drop in temperature. If the cellar has no windows, the door should be left open, but only for as long as the temperature can be maintained.

Because most cellars are below ground level, they are not directly affected by the extreme fluctuations of temperature outside. Overheating in summer or chilling in winter are therefore unlikely. The lighting equipment is usually sufficient to maintain an even temperature, making other forms of heating unnecessary, although this will depend upon the ratio of lights to volume of space, of course. Three or four tiers of shelving against the walls, each with its own battery of lights, in a cellar the size of a small room, will probably generate too much heat, making some form of extraction necessary.

Indoor growing cases

It is a common mistake to enclose orchids in a mini-greenhouse made from bamboo canes and polythene which is barely large enough for the plants at their present size, and certainly allows no room for future growth. Like oversized fish in a small bowl, these plants are doomed to failure, through lack of the all important supply of fresh air. Equally disastrous can be the use of small propagators. These units are designed for germinating bedding plants and raising fast growing vegetable seedlings, as well as cuttings etc., but should not be considered as permanent homes for adult plants, still less a place to grow your orchids! The largest of the propagators may be suitable for the smaller growing orchids, although they hardly present an attractive feature for the home.

When your small orchid collection has outgrown the window sill and you wish to progress further, taking the art of orchid growing more seriously, better results will be achieved by placing your orchids in a proper orchid case, designed specifically for that purpose and providing a permanent indoor home for your orchids. The first people to successfully grow tropical plants indoors were the Victorians. In the large, spacious rooms of their houses they were never without a space in which to grow their palms, potted ferns and others, which were the forerunners of the modern house plant. It was to be expected that when the cultivation of orchids became fashionable they desired to grow these indoors as well. Indeed, some plants thrived extremely well. *Paphiopedilum insigne* was one example which could be grown into large specimen plants and was not an uncommon sight on Victorian window sills. This tolerant plant could withstand any amount of neglect or overindulgence by its owner. Its amazing vigour would sustain it for many years and it would bloom throughout the decades in spite of the conditions, rather than because of them. It is not unusual to find these same plants growing today having been passed down from generation to generation!

Wardian Cases
Much of this early culture of tropical plants was achieved by growing them in Wardian Cases. These were large, glass fronted boxes which could be placed more or less anywhere in a well lit area of the drawing room and in which the plants would thrive. Inside the case humidity could be maintained to create the moisture necessary for the plants' health. It is interesting that the Wardian Case originated as a glass structure built on the open decks of the early sailing ships. The object was to preserve living plants in transit from their country of origin. The earlier practice was to dry the plants and pack them into crates placed in the hold of the ship. This crude method resulted in tremendous losses to the plants; many thousands rotted in the holds during the weeks at sea and only a small percentage survived the journey. It was thought that by replacing this method with the Wardian Case the plants' chances of survival would be increased and the losses reduced. Unfortunately this idea was not a success and was soon abandoned. However, the Wardian Case was not completely discarded and found favour as a method of displaying the fabled orchids in the drawing room. Often the plants would be grown in large humid greenhouses and then brought into the case for the duration of their blooming period. These cases went out of fashion as the Victorian era declined and the large estates on which the orchids were grown were broken up.

Wardian Cases, first designed to hold plants during transit on ships, later became fashionable for the growing of indoor plants. They were modified to blend in with the furniture of that age.

Modern cases

However, the growing of orchids in a small way as a hobby began to gain in popularity and escalated during the first half of the twentieth century. This was mainly due to the improvement of small greenhouse construction and better heating arrangements combined with the availability of cheap coal. Fewer plants were grown indoors as gardeners were generally content to grow their orchids in greenhouses, which at that time, before the advent of modern central heating, were more suitable than homes. However, with the increase in centrally heated houses and large windowed, gardenless flats, the culture of house plants, including orchids, enjoyed an unprecedented revival. Nowhere was this trend more evident than on the continent of Europe where house plants and cut flowers became immensely popular and were regarded as an important feature of any room. To keep up with this new demand, the number of commercial growers increased dramatically.

Once again there arose a demand for a case similar to the once popular Wardian Case. The modern equivalents are called indoor greenhouses or planteriums, and bear little resemblance to the original Wardian Case. Although both were designed for holding plants, the modern planterium is built to house orchids permanently, catering for their every need, while the Wardian Case was mainly intended to hold plants in flower creating a short term display. The modern case, beautifully finished and pleasing to the eye becomes a piece of furniture in the room. They are obtainable in a number of materials including various coloured woods to suit decor, or stainless steel for office or hotel lounge. The main features are the large sliding glass doors and glass sides which allow an uninterrupted view of the flowers inside. The bottom section of the case consists of a watertight fibreglass tray concealed in the base, which may be 12–15 cm (5–6 in.) deep. This can be filled with any suitable material such as expanded clay pellets, granulated bark or gravel. Clay pellets are ideal for this purpose; they are very light, clean and pleasing to look at. However, if these are unavailable, granulated bark, as used in potting, gravel or coloured chippings may be used as good substitutes. This material is kept permanently moist to provide the necessary humidity for the case. Laid in the tray and out of sight is the heating cable. This is controlled by a thermostat and maintains the required temperature inside the case independent of the temperature in the room outside.

If the case is standing by a large and well lit window there may be no need for artificial lighting. However, in many rooms it is found that the most appropriate position is far away from any window, often in a dark corner. Here artificial lighting can be used with complete success enabling the plants to be viewed at their best. Tube lighting concealed in the roof of the case will ensure that the plants not only look well but also flourish under these conditions. The best form of lighting equipment uses fluorescent tubes of high output, and manufacturers are continually producing new types, improving them all the time. Always be sure to use only tubes which have been specifically designed for plants.

It is important that these lights should be in use every day to give the plants the equivalent of the daylight hours they require. This can only really be achieved using a time switch ensuring a regular cycle of light and dark. This cycle can be adjusted to fit in with the use of the room; the orchid 'day' can be continued well into the evening so that the display may be enjoyed by all. The time switch can also be linked to the thermostat to give a variation in temperature between the periods of light and dark.

Slots for ventilation are incorporated in the top and bottom of most cases allowing a movement of air around the plants. For additional freshness a small electric fan can be installed and the glass doors can be opened for a few hours each day, providing a change of air at least once every twenty-four hours.

In combined rooms, such as kitchen/dining rooms, a case can be incorporated into the room divider so that it can be viewed from both sides. In this situation the case would need to have all glass sides, but for a case standing close to a wall, a background is necessary. Some models have a fibreglass back which can be painted to suit the decor of the room. Free standing cases can be mounted on castors making them mobile to a certain extent so that they can be pulled out for cleaning or moved from one room to another. This is also an advantage should you move house.

Window cases

A further variation on the indoor greenhouse theme is possible if you have a suitable bay, or deeply recessed window. With the construction of a second, inner window across the recess, an attractive growing area is formed, enclosed in glass. In many older houses such windows may provide a growing space over 50 cm (18 in.) deep. Provided that the outside window is double glazed and a heating system is installed similar to that mentioned for cases, an excellent growing and display area will be obtained. No artificial light will be required for growing the plants here as there should be sufficient natural light. In fact, if the window receives long periods of bright sunlight during the summer, it will be necessary to provide some form of shading such as Venetian blinds or net curtains, together with adequate ventilation to prevent the area overheating. The aspect of the window must be considered to ensure that your plants receive enough light during winter without scorching in summer. A west or east facing window should have just about the right amount of light.

Ventilation may be obtained by opening either the inside or outside windows and an automatic ventilation arm can be installed if the grower is away from the house all day. One of the greatest dangers from this method of growing orchids is that the humidity created for the plants may cause dampness to seep through the walls of the house. The walls should be painted with a sealing compound to prevent this.

Care and cleaning

The care of your built-in windows or orchid case is most important to the success of your plants. There are a number of jobs which should become routine, such as the daily spraying and weekly watering of the plants. Each day the plants should be lightly sprayed, and the base medium well wetted to maintain a moist humid atmosphere in the case.

It is important that whatever material is used for the base, it should be kept wet at all times to provide this all important humidity. The water level in the base tray should be maintained at half the depth of the gravel and should not be allowed to rise above this to avoid the danger of spillage onto the carpets. Your reservoir of water will slowly be evaporating and should be replaced with the surplus water from watering and spraying.

At least once a year it will become necessary to remove the plants from the case in order to clean it. The base material should be taken out and thrown away, if decomposable, or washed, if gravel. The tray should then be cleaned with Jeyes Fluid before fresh base material is put in. When this has been done, the plants should be examined carefully to make sure that they are healthy and free from pests. Check the undersides of the leaves and behind the sheaths thoroughly for signs of insect pests. If necessary, the plants can be repotted before they are returned to the case. The arrangement in the case will probably have to be changed, as you will find that some plants have grown more than others and it is best to place the largest to the back with the shorter ones in front. This makes watering easier and allows each plant to be shown off to its best advantage. The plants to the rear may be placed on inverted flower pots to give height, while those towards the front can be plunged into the base medium, but no deeper than the water level to avoid drowning the roots.

Selection of plants
The addition of a few foliage plants nicely placed among the orchids can greatly enhance the display. Beware of the fast growing types which will overtake the orchids in no time and dominate the whole case. Choose instead from a number of pretty, slow growing varieties such as members of the Bromeliaceae (pineapple) family (e.g. tillansias), miniature ferns and palms or the small, creeping coelogynella, which makes an ideal cover for the base. These additions not only help to create an interesting display but will ensure the development of a good microclimate in your tropical garden.

A carefully chosen selection of orchids will ensure flowers all the year round. Choose long lasting or continuously flowering varieties so that whatever the season you will have orchids in bloom. Another consideration is to select good looking plants, and plants with attractive evergreen foliage which do not become eyesores when out of bloom.

The value of an artificially controlled growing area is that it is completely independent of the elements. The seasons and daylight hours can be adjusted according to the needs of the plants and yourself.

65

Temperature and humidity

When orchids are grown in an open room, it is a mistake to expect them to sit on the window sill or coffee table and simply 'get on with it'. The plants must rely upon the care and assistance of their owner to keep them in good health. They will require regular and correct amounts of water with special attention to temperature and humidity.

Most of the cultivated orchids are epiphytes which grow, in the wild, on the branches of trees in humid, tropical countries. Along with other plants such as mosses, lichens and ferns, their roots are continually moist through being exposed to the air. When growing orchids in the home,

Humidity is very important for orchids. Plants should be grown over a trough of gravel which is kept permanently wet. The water level should not be allowed to rise above the gravel surface.

these conditions should be recreated as nearly as possible. If they are not in a case, each plant should be placed on an upturned half pot standing in a saucer filled with gravel. The gravel should be kept permanently wet, causing humid air to rise around the plant. Moisture will percolate up through the holes in the pot and be drawn upwards in a chimney action through the compost.

Where several plants are grown together the principle remains the same but the method is enlarged, using troughs to hold several plants. The more plants that you grow in close proximity to each other in this way, the greater is their surrounding microclimate. There is a whole range of decorative plant troughs, from inexpensive plastic containers to shiny copper types, all suitable for a few orchid plants.

66

A constant check on the temperature is essential and one should always have a minimum/maximum thermometer close to the plants. These are easily obtainable for a small outlay from any garden shop. All plants have a wide temperature tolerance which can range from 7–10°C (45–50°F) at night, to over 24°C (75°F) in the daytime. Modern thermostatically controlled central heating has made it easier to grow plants in the home but it must be remembered that a comfortable 18–22°C (65–70°F) day and night with little variation will not suit all varieties. Some of the cooler growing types do better with an open fire which is lit only during the day and evening, benefiting from the regular variation in temperature.

Compost
Orchids grow in a compost which is totally different from that of any other plant. Bearing in mind that most of the cultivated orchids are epiphytes or have epiphytic ancestors they are not going to thrive in a general pot plant compost. Orchids prefer a coarse organic compost through which their thick roots can travel easily. In their natural environment the wild plants growing upon the trees have their roots in contact with the bark, mosses and any plant debris lodged in the branches of the host tree. In cultivation the grower is obliged to produce a compost as close to this as possible, made up from materials which are locally available.

In different parts of the world it is possible to obtain from orchid nurseries a variety of tree barks which form the basis of the best modern orchid composts. While granulated bark chippings form the most suitable base material, bark on its own makes a very dry compost which will not retain sufficient moisture for the plants. A small quantity of peat should therefore be mixed in and a few charcoal chunks added to keep the compost sweet. Peat should not be used on its own, as it can quickly become sodden and sour, to the detriment of the roots. If bark is not available, a mixture of peat and charcoal with granulated polystyrene or coarse sand as an aggregate is a suitable substitute. The first requirement of any orchid compost is that it should be well drained and water should flow through it without becoming clogged. Other materials such as oak leaves or chopped bracken can be successfully used for orchids, but these take longer to prepare and decompose more quickly than the bark or peat, in which a plant may remain for several years before the compost breaks down. The compost must be able to sustain a plant for at least two years, otherwise it could be argued that lawn mowings would make a suitable compost, being an organic material made up of leaves. But, of course,

67

these are green leaves, which decompose extremely quickly and would be most detrimental to the roots.

Rather than experimenting with various composts, the beginner would be well advised to purchase suitably prepared compost from a commercial orchid nursery which has probably spent years perfecting its own type of compost. The professional growers' experience can be relied on to ensure that you are using the best compost for your orchids. However, if you are unable to obtain compost this way and need to make your own, then a good guide using materials available from most garden shops would be a mixture of coarse sphagnum peat, having first sifted out the dust, and best potting sand as used by cacti growers. The ratio of sand to peat can vary according to the individual growers' needs. The grower who tends to overwater his or her plants should use more sand, while the grower who has little time for watering should use less sand to keep his plants moist for longer periods.

Watering

Frequency and amount
There is no hard and fast rule that can be laid down for watering orchids. It depends on so many variables such as the species, size and stage of orchid, the size of pot, density of compost, humidity and temperature. A large, actively growing plant in a small pot may need soaking twice a week or more. Each plant should therefore be examined daily, lifting it to see if it feels light compared with when it was last watered. The surface of the compost may appear dry while the material underneath is still quite moist, particularly if standing in a fairly deep humidity tray. Only experience will teach you when to water by comparing wet and dry plants. A dry plant with shrivelled bulbs is a sure sign of underwatering, but a thorough soaking will soon restore the bulbs to a plump and healthy state. No growing plant should be allowed to become dry for any length of time and it should be remembered that plants growing indoors will dry out much quicker than those in a greenhouse where the humidity is high.

Certain orchids, such as the Cattleyas and Dendrobiums, have a definite growing and resting cycle. Many do not grow during the winter and show little sign of root activity or new leaf production. During this resting period the plant will require less frequent watering than when growing and only sufficient to prevent the bulbs shrivelling should be given. The deciduous Pleiones and some of the Lycastes have a much deeper resting period, losing their leaves completely when the season's growth is complete, leaving only the bulbs to carry them through the winter months. These orchids should not be given any water at all until their new growths appear. It will be found that they can go for many weeks without water with no shrivelling of the bulbs, providing they are healthy and plump at the start of the resting season. Indoor orchids are not as strongly affected by the seasons as those grown in greenhouses. The more constant temperature lessens the seasonal change and the cycle of a recently acquired plant will gradually change as it adapts to its new environment.

Orchids such as Paphiopedilums and Phalaenopsis do not have pseudo bulbs and therefore have no large food reserves to sustain them through a resting period. These plants are continuously growing and should be kept evenly moist all the year round. You will probably find that during the winter months when the room is artificially heated, the atmosphere is much drier and the plants may require more frequent watering.

Bulbous orchids such as Cymbidiums and Odontoglossum hybrids are continuously growing and require little or no resting. They can be treated as recommended for the Phalaenopsis and Paphiopedilums. By comparing the new bulb with that produced in the previous year, one can tell when the plant has reached the stage in its cycle where less water will be required until once again the new growth is visible at the base. The length of this time will vary from genus to genus. Again, careful observation will indicate what is required by the individual plant.

Method
When watering plants in the home it is a good idea to take them to the kitchen if possible. They can then be placed on the draining board and the compost thoroughly flooded without fear of damaging carpets or furniture. Dry bark is liable to float away and so it is best to immerse the whole pot in a bowl of water, raising the level of the water to a fraction below the rim of the pot. After soaking for about 15 minutes, the plant can be drained and returned to its growing position. This procedure should be repeated regularly to ensure that all the compost is thoroughly soaked. A small trickle of water now and again when you think about it, is not sufficient; it will quickly run through without saturating the compost. An orchid grown in the correct compost cannot easily be over-watered; the material is so open that any surface water quickly drains away. A wet, but well ventilated compost suits orchids best. Of course some plants will be too large to carry to the kitchen. These are best

watered with a can where they stand; the surface of the compost being thoroughly flooded several times to ensure saturation.

Water quality
The quality of domestic water supply varies tremendously from area to area and this is an important consideration when it is to be used for watering orchids. The pH is particularly important and should ideally be on the acidic side at a value of about pH 5. Very hard water is not good for orchids but beware of chemical water softeners; these introduce chemicals just as injurious to your plants as the hardness. The householder can collect rain water from the roof if this is preferred to the domestic supply, but if you live in an upstairs flat you will have no choice other than to use water from the tap. In this case, if you find that the water is hard and alkaline, a harmless method of softening is to suspend a nylon mesh bag full of peat in a bucket of the water for a few days. This will absorb much of the lime content and lower the pH. Whatever the source of the water, it should always be given to the plants at room temperature. It is always a good idea to fill the watering can the day before it is to be used, to allow the temperature to adjust and unwanted chemicals to settle.

One of the advantages of growing orchids indoors is that they can be watered at any time of the day to suit your own convenience. In a greenhouse more careful attention is required to water on a rising temperature and never in extremely cold weather when the temperature is below the recommended minimum. In the home, where a more comfortable climate exists, no harm will come to the plants if the watering is done in the morning or evening.

Feeding
To achieve perfection with your orchids, proper feeding is essential. Any properly watered plant which is growing well, with new growths and an active root system, should be fed. The grower has many different fertilisers to choose from, and a visit to your local garden shop will reveal a whole range of plant foods available. If you already have a preference for a particular feed with which you are familiar, use this for your orchids. There are very few feeds produced especially for orchids, and any good plant fertiliser may be used at the strength recommended on the label. Bearing in mind that orchids are slow growing plants, the feed should be given at the weakest recommended dose.

70

If you use a liquid feed, this may be given at the time of watering. Start to feed your orchids when the new growths are a few inches high, and from then on apply at every other watering throughout the growing season. Some fertilisers may be used as a foliar feed, applied to the plant as a spray at least once a week. Do not allow foliar feed to fall directly onto buds or flowers. Plants with extremely delicate foliage, such as the Lycastes, are better not foliar fed as this will cause the leaves to become spotted. Feed for these orchids should only be applied when watering. A plant which is resting may need a little water to keep its bulbs plump, but it should not be fed during this time, nor should a plant which has been neglected and is not in good health until it has made a new root system capable of taking up the fertiliser. Correct feeding will result in a strong healthy plant which will produce better flowers and continue to grow for many years at perfection.

Repotting and dividing

Because of their slow rate of growth compared with most other types of house plants, orchids are seldom potted more than once a year, and are very often left for two years before it is necessary to disturb them. However, certainly after two years the compost will have broken down and need replacing as the food value becomes exhausted, the plant will have outgrown the pot, and its roots will have become potbound.

There are several indications that a plant is in need of repotting. The compost may be decomposed and this can be determined by pushing a finger into it. If this can be done easily the compost needs replacing and the plant should be repotted. If the leading bulb has reached the rim of the pot or is protruding over the edge leaving no room for future growth inside the pot, or if the plant has pushed itself up above the pot rim, it has outgrown its pot. The foliage may have turned a yellow green which indicates starvation, the food in the compost having been used up. Bulbless orchids such as Paphiopedilums or Phalaenopsis, which do not progress across the pot in the same way as those with a horizontal rhizome, are best repotted when their roots have filled the pot, or are showing above the rim.

For most orchids the best time of the year to repot is usually the spring when the new growth is quite young. New roots always follow the new growth and it is best to repot just before the roots start growing. Repotting is beneficial to the plant and the new roots will quickly gain nourishment from the new compost.

Repotting methods
There are two methods of repotting; the first, known as 'dropping on', can be done when a plant needs nothing removing and the compost has not deteriorated to any extent. The plant is simply removed from its pot and placed in a slightly larger one without any disturbance to the existing root ball. The space between the root ball and pot sides is filled with fresh compost, which must be of the same mixture as previously used, and firmed down with the fingers. This method of repotting is the easiest for the beginner and can often be applied to orchids purchased from commercial nurseries when you can enquire about their last repotting. Dropping on the same plant should not be repeated for more than a few years. After a time the compost at the centre of the root ball will be several years old and will have decomposed considerably. Also, the older roots will have died and should be removed. Complete repotting therefore becomes essential after a few years. This involves the removal of all old compost, dead roots and bulbs and any surplus bulbs which are becoming a burden on the plant. It is much more of an upheaval than dropping on, for the plant as well as for the novice grower!

Preparation
When preparing to repot your first orchids give yourself as large a working area as possible, making sure you have all the necessary materials close to hand. You will need a supply of fresh compost, previously moistened, a supply of crocking material, a selection of flower pots of the anticipated sizes, slow release fertiliser such as bone meal or hoof and horn to be sprinkled in the base, and a pair of sharp secateurs.

The plant should not be watered for several days prior to repotting. It can then be removed from its pot by turning it upside down and carefully tapping the edge of the pot on the worktop. Support the plant with one hand and after a few taps it should come loose. Be careful not to damage the new growths while doing this; the plant should be held so that they are away from the worktop. Plants which are extremely rootbound do not always come out of their pot very easily and it may sometimes be necessary to resort to breaking the pot. Plastic pots can be cut away, while a clay pot will have to be broken with a small hammer.

BASIC STEPS IN REPOTTING ORCHIDS

These illustrations show a Cattleya in the various stages of being repotted. This method can be followed for any bulbous or bulbless orchid.

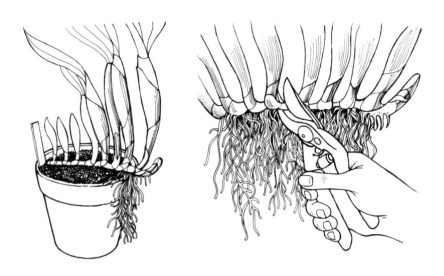

1. Our example is of an extremely potbound plant which has not been repotted for three years. The compost has deteriorated so that it no longer retains any food value but the plant continues to flourish, maintaining itself on reserves in the bulbs and absorbing moisture from the air through its aerial roots. Even so, it should have been repotted last season. To the left (the rear of the plant) are the older, leafless bulbs. These are joined to the mature, flowered bulbs which still carry their foliage, and at the front the new growth can be seen, with its young roots. Repotting should be done while the new roots are short, to avoid damage.
2. Remove the plant from its pot by turning it upside down and tapping out. If the roots are attached firmly to the sides, it may be necessary to break the pot. Shake out all loose compost and untangle the roots. Any excess leafless bulbs which are performing no useful function, should now be removed by severing the rhizome between two bulbs with a pair of secateurs or a sharp pruning knife. Ensure that at least four good bulbs remain to support the plant. Some of the removed back bulbs may be repotted singly and grown on as propagations. However, these will take many years to reach flowering size.

73

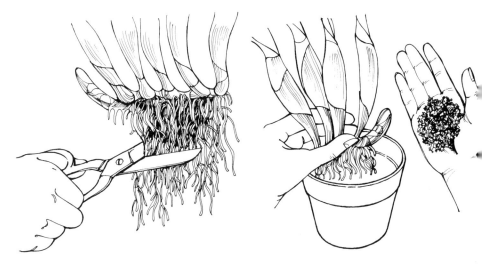

3. *Depending on their condition, the roots will need removing or trimming. Those which are obviously dead should be cut back close to the rhizome. Trim long, living roots to a convenient length, usually about 10 cm (4 in.) leaving sufficient length to form an anchorage in the new compost. Take care not to damage the roots at the base of the new growth.*

4. *Choice of pot size is important. The new pot should give the plant just sufficient room for a further two or three bulbs. After removal of back bulbs it may return to the same or even smaller size of pot. Overpotting should be avoided as it leads to overwatering. Having selected a pot, place crocking in the bottom to allow drainage. Position the plant with the severed end of the rhizome against the rim of the pot and the new growth slightly below the opposite rim. This is the correct final position. Remove the plant and place sufficient compost in the bottom so that when the plant is returned it rests on the compost in the right position.*

5. *Supporting the plant with its roots tucked underneath it, fill in with compost, firming down each handful. Use the fingers to work the compost around the sides of the pot, taking care not to push against the plant. When half full, a pinch of slow release fertiliser, such as bone meal or hoof and horn, may be sprinkled evenly round the pot. Continue to add compost until the surface is just below the pot rim. The plant should now be firmly supported by the compost although large, heavy plants may require the additional support of a cane until their new roots have grown.*
6. *The new growth should be on a level with the surface of the compost. In some cases, where a plant has grown upwards as well as forwards, it may be necessary to partially bury the older bulbs to achieve this. If the plant has ended up too high above the surface, it will be unable to make a new root system quickly and it is best to remove the plant and start again with a little less compost under the plant. Replace the label with the date of repotting. The plant should be sprayed regularly for several days, but not watered until the roots have healed. In three or four days begin to water sparingly and resume normal watering after a further week.*

Root health

Having removed the plant from its pot now is the best opportunity to carefully examine the roots. A great deal can be learnt about the health of your plants by the condition of the roots. They should be abundant, penetrating the compost evenly to the bottom of the pot, and should be white in most cases, alive and healthy. The compost may be decomposed and bear little resemblance to its original form especially if the plant has not been touched for several years. Where a plant is not too rootbound the old compost will shake off quite easily with a little help from the fingers working the compost loose from in between the roots. It is often surprising to find how long the roots are when they become unwound, and these will have to be trimmed back to a convenient length for easy insertion in the new pot. It is a mistake to wind long living roots into the base of the new pot; these will be too easily broken and a rot will set up in the breaks as soon as watering begins. Therefore these long, brittle roots will benefit from trimming back and on a healthy vigorous plant they will be replaced in no time.

There will undoubtedly be a number of dead roots from the oldest parts of the plant, which will not be immediately apparent, but will show up as the old compost is removed. These appear brown and lifeless, and the old outer covering can be peeled off, leaving the thin wire core of the root exposed. They should be completely removed at their base. A few dead roots are to be expected; like the leaves, roots live for a few years and are then replaced by new ones from the younger growth. So, provided these dead roots are in the minority and come from the oldest growth, all is well. However, should the number of dead roots exceed live ones or if all the roots are dead, there is something wrong with your culture. Dead roots will almost certainly mean shrivelled bulbs, as they will have been unable to obtain moisture and a quick look will confirm this. The loss of roots in this way is nearly always caused by overwatering which has simply drowned the roots. This can be confirmed by the state of the compost which will, in these circumstances, be very wet and soggy. If it can be taken in the hand and water squeezed from it then it has become waterlogged. Healthy orchid roots cannot stand compost in this state for long, bearing in mind that in their natural habitat they would be creeping along the bark of a tree, often fully exposed to the air. Should all the roots be dead, allow just sufficient to remain on the plant to act as anchorage in the new compost and throw away the old compost and severed roots, taking care not to get them mixed with the fresh compost.

76

Dividing and back bulb removal

If required, the plant may now be divided or have a few of its back bulbs removed. The back bulbs are the oldest and leafless bulbs which have discarded their foliage and have been supporting the younger bulbs and their new growths. These bulbs are of great benefit and should not be removed unless they outnumber the green bulbs in leaf. In this case the excess back bulbs become an encumbrance to the plant and should be removed to restore the balance of the plant. A plant which is growing in more than one direction, as indicated by the new growths, may be large enough for division into two plants if at least four bulbs, including both green and leafless bulbs, can be retained on each piece. The pseudo bulbs are joined together by a hard woody rhizome which is visible on Cattleyas, for example, but hidden on Cymbidiums and Odontoglossums. In the latter its position can be determined by gently pressing the bulbs apart. To divide a plant or remove an unwanted back bulb this rhizome must be cleanly severed with a sharp knife or pair of secateurs. As a general rule for most of the bulbous orchids, never reduce a plant or divide it to less than four good bulbs, otherwise it will be greatly weakened and will take several years to restore itself to flowering size. However, there are a few exceptions, such as the Pleiones, where the old bulb decomposes quickly and plants never consist of more than one green bulb each year.

For the bulbless orchids, if it is necessary to divide a very large Paphiopedilum, the rhizome should be severed between the growths leaving at least four growths on each division.

The old back bulbs removed from Cattleyas and Cymbidiums will start new growths if potted up singly, and if grown for several years will produce further flowering sized plants. However, whether one is prepared to give up space for several years to a non-flowering plant identical to one already flowering, is a matter of personal choice. In a greenhouse these plants can be grown to flowering size within three or four years, but indoors, they may take as long as six or seven years, during which time they require as much care and attention as flowering plants, but with less immediate reward to the grower.

Repotting

Having seen to the roots and bulbs, the prepared plant is now ready to be returned to its pot. Plastic pots are recommended for indoor orchids as they have many advantages over the old clay pots. They are cleaner and lighter to handle and do not absorb water; all the water given to the plant goes into the compost. The open bark mix required by orchids will dry out very quickly in a clay pot making it extremely difficult to keep sufficiently moist.

Not all plants will need a larger pot after repotting. Some, such as the Paphiopedilums, will require little if any root trimming and, after shaking off the old compost, they can be happily returned to their old pot. They rarely make sufficient roots to fill their pot as do other orchids. Plants which have been reduced in size by the removal of unwanted pseudo bulbs may well fit in the same size pot as before, and divisions will probably need smaller pots. The correct size is judged by placing the plant in the pot with the oldest bulbs against the rim. There should be just sufficient room in front of the plant for a further two years' growth before it will again reach the pot rim. If the container is considered too small then a larger one must be found, but it is a mistake to overpot and nothing looks worse than a small plant in an oversized pot surrounded by an expanse of compost. Overpotting also leads to overwatering, so be on the safe side and use as small a pot as possible, leaving just sufficient space as described.

Some form of drainage will be necessary at the bottom of the pot. This may be whatever is available to you, broken pot shards or broken polystyrene tiles make an ideal drainage. Just sufficient is required to cover the bottom of the pot. On top of the drainage crocking is placed a layer of compost. This layer should be deep enough to enable the plant to be placed so that the base of the leading growth is level with, or a fraction below, the rim of the pot. Some orchids have a tendency to grow upwards, each bulb being made slightly above the previous one. In this case it may be necessary to bury the oldest bulbs to bring the leading bulb into position. With its roots tucked underneath its bulbs the plant can be held in place with one hand, while compost is poured in with the other, until all the space is filled. It is important to work the compost in evenly all round the sides, particularly round the back, to ensure that there are no cavities left around the roots. The compost is then pressed down with the fingers; a potting stick is not necessary, and it should be possible to get the compost firm enough to hold the plant stable. When the pot is half full some growers like to add a pinch or two of bone meal or hoof and horn to act as a slow release fertiliser. If used, it should be restricted to a pinch, as harm can be done to new roots through burning if this is overdone. The compost should finish just below the rim of the pot to allow for future watering. For reference it is always a good idea to make a record of the potting date on the label, and whether the plant was dropped on or repotted.

78

Repotting bulbless orchids
Bulbless orchids such as Phalaenopsis and Paphiopedilums should be repotted in exactly the same way as orchids with bulbs although there will be little old material to be removed and very little trimming of the roots should be necessary. You may find that your Phalaenopsis plants have produced extensive aerial roots outside the pot. This is quite natural and it is a mistake to try and force these into the new pot. If compared with the roots inside the pot, it will be seen they are different in appearance and they will suffocate if buried. If any of them are dead or have become broken they should be shortened for the sake of appearance. This will not harm the plant which will very quickly make new ones. Repot the plant leaving the exposed roots outside the pot.

Care
The immediate after care of a newly potted plant is important. No matter how carefully you have handled the plant, the disturbance will have been a shock to its system. Nevertheless, repotting is beneficial to the plant and with the right attention it will soon respond by making new roots. For the first two days after repotting the plant is better left dry to allow any damage to the roots to heal and prevent any rot setting in. During this period the plant may be sprayed or the leaves wiped with a damp sponge to keep them fresh.

Care of foliage and flowers
Like everything in the home, your house plants will become dusty, and orchids are no exception. An accumulation of fine dust building up on the surface of the leaves will, if left for a long period, prevent the leaves from breathing properly and will impede the light which is so essential for a healthy plant. Periodically, at least once a month, this dust should be cleaned off using a wet sponge and a bowl of clean water, wiping each leaf and the stems and bulbs. The leaves can then be passed under a running tap. This will not only greatly benefit the plant but will also improve its appearance. Flowers and buds should not be dusted, these should be left well alone for fear of bruising.

Spraying
Many orchids enjoy a daily spraying of their foliage. In the home this is difficult for obvious reasons, but if the plant is removed from the growing area for regular watering, spraying could be carried out at the same time. Where plants are grown in a sun room or conservatory the culture

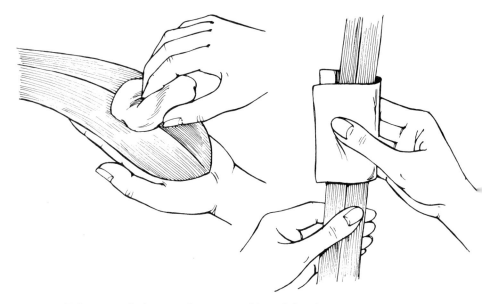

Foliage must be kept as clean as possible and free from dust. Regular sponging will keep the leaves healthy and glossy.

a) *The broad foliage of a Phalaenopsis, Cattleya or Paphiopedilum should be supported underneath while a wet sponge is drawn forward along the leaf. Do not use a backward and forward scrubbing movement. After washing, the leaf may be dried with a paper tissue using the same method. Be careful to avoid cracking or splitting the fleshy leaves. It will not be necessary with these orchids to sponge the undersides of the leaves.*

b) *The long leaves of orchids such as Cymbidiums and Odontoglossums can be cleaned on both sides. While the base of the leaf is held with one hand, a wet sponge or paper tissue wrapped loosely round the leaf should be drawn along towards the top. This can be repeated several times until all dust is removed. This procedure will also remove pests such as red spider mite which may be present on the underside of the leaves. Only the leaves on mature bulbs should be cleaned in this way; leaves on immature young growths will all too easily be pulled away from the tender base.*

will resemble that in a greenhouse. On hot sunny days plants like Cymbidiums will benefit from a thorough overhead spray, and the floor and the staging may be wetted to produce extra humidity. Plants in orchid cases or over humidity trays can be sprayed and the gravel at their base should be kept permanently moist. If you are attempting cellar cultivation, regular damping down to improve the atmosphere should be a routine job. With greenhouse culture of orchids, spraying is restricted to the summer months, the greenhouse being more affected by the seasonal fluctuations and adverse weather in the winter. Plants in the home are far less aware of the outdoor extremes and may be sprayed all the year round; even a resting plant will benefit from having its foliage moistened regularly.

Care and display of blooms
The care and display of the blooms produced as a result of years of careful nurture, is all part of home orchid growing. To show off the blooms to their best advantage the flower spikes will require some form of support, bearing in mind that many of them will hold their flowers for many weeks. Cymbidiums, Odontoglossums and Phalaenopsis are all spray orchids producing long stems of flowers which will require some support. A thin bamboo cane should be inserted into the pot, close to the plant and away from the rim of the pot where the majority of the roots are. To this the growing spike can be loosely tied up to the base of the buds. The flowers can be allowed to arch naturally. Young flower spikes are extremely brittle and can be all too easily snapped. The supporting cane will ensure protection as well as giving support. Paphiopedilums will benefit from a stake with a single tie just behind the flower, but this should not be applied until the stem is fully grown and the single bud has opened and is mature. The long caned Dendrobiums which bloom along their length in clusters or small panicles will require their bulbs supported in an upright position, while the flowers are left free. After flowering, the spikes on the spray orchids should be cut about 2 cm (1 in.) from the base of the plant and the supporting cane removed. The cane should always be as short as possible, cutting off any surplus above the buds. A tall length of unwanted cane looks unsightly and can be dangerous when handling the plant.

If you prefer your flowering orchids to remain in their growing positions while in bloom, the spikes can be cut and placed in another room for display. They will last just as long in water as on the plant. This not only allows the plant to stay in a good growing position but also takes

81

the strain from the plant at a time when the new growth is starting. The flower spikes on Phalaenopsis are the exception here; it will be seen that there are several 'eyes' along the length of stem between the base and the flowers. If the spike is cut back to one of these eyes a further spray of blooms will result. This action is only recommended on a strong, healthy plant which can support its blooms over several months.

Common problems

Pests
Plants indoors have the advantage of growing in isolated conditions maintaining little contact with the outside world; this means that they are not generally troubled with the typical insect pests. Plants growing in the garden are subjected to a continual bombardment from a variety of insect pests which have to be constantly combated with insecticides to protect the plants. Greenhouse plants are likewise affected, often more so in the artificially warm conditions created for them which provide an ideal habitat for garden pests. Every type of pest from slugs and snails to greenfly and red spider mite can establish itself in the greenhouse from the garden outside.

In the home the plants are separated from all these problems, and there should be no need to resort to the modern chemical insecticides. Because they can be dangerous and quite unsuitable for use indoors, insecticides are not recommended for orchids in the home. Far safer, and often just as effective, is a box of tissues and plenty of clean water. Ideally you should start with clean healthy plants, and provided your orchids have been obtained from a reliable source, the plants should be free from any insect pests.

By their nature orchids do not make very good hosts for a variety of predators; their tough foliage makes them undesirable to many of the common or garden pests. Greenfly could possibly gain access to your orchids during the summer through open windows, but even so they seldom attack orchid leaves except some of the varieties with the most delicate annual foliage, or possibly tender young growths. If greenfly are apparent, they will almost certainly be found on the young buds or flowers. Regular inspection of developing buds will soon detect this pest which is not difficult to see with the naked eye. These aphids have one of the fastest breeding rates of all insects and they spread quickly, building up into colonies if allowed to remain unrestricted. The greenfly is a sap sucking predator which pierces the surface of the buds causing deformity

82

of the cells which becomes more pronounced as the buds become larger. When the flower opens it is greatly disfigured with blotching and twisting of the sepals and petals. If the greenfly attack has been severe and unchecked the buds will turn yellow and drop off without opening.

At the first sign of a few greenfly it is sufficient to wipe them off between finger and thumb or using a piece of cotton wool. If the greenfly can be seen in and around a tight cluster of buds too small to be handled, they may be dislodged with the aid of a small paint brush. Alternatively, the buds can be immersed in a bowl of water and swilled gently round until the pest is dislodged. The water should be used at room temperature, and the surplus shaken from the buds. A further examination the next day to ensure that no aphids were missed or have since hatched is all that is needed to prevent further trouble. This method of control is far better where just a few aphids are noticed than immediate spraying with insecticide which, if directed onto soft buds, can do further damage by burning.

Red spider mite is well known to any gardener. It will attack a whole range of plants both out of doors and in the greenhouse. It is a most persistent and extremely small mite which usually requires the aid of a magnifying glass to see it at all. On orchids it will first attack the undersides of the leaves where a silvery pattern can be detected on the surface. This damage is caused by the mite piercing the leaf, killing the leaf cells, and these areas will spread if the pest remains undetected. Eventually, the white areas turn brown and black as a result of secondary infection feeding on the dead leaf cells. The best method of prevention and control indoors is regular sponging of the leaves using a moist, white paper tissue. On Cymbidiums the leaf should be supported at its base with one hand, while the tissue is run the length of the leaf held between finger and thumb. Inspection of the tissue will easily reveal any red spider mite although it may again be necessary to use a magnifying glass for this purpose.

Two further pests which are traditionally troublesome to orchids are scale insects and mealy bug. These are usually introduced into a collection on freshly imported species and sometimes remain undetected, concealed beneath the sheaths of Cattleyas and similar orchids. The scale insect is as its common name describes; it may be round or oval shaped and usually lives in clusters on the less accessible parts of the plant. The mealy bug is white, and covers itself in a powdery substance. It frequents similar parts of the plant as the scale insect. Both these pests are large enough to be seen with the naked eye, although they may have to be searched for, especially around the base of the plant. They both thrive in a dry atmosphere and can build up into large colonies. If allowed to grow unchecked they will slowly sap the strength of the plant, weakening it and eventually causing its death. These pests can be all too easily missed when sponging the leaves, and in searching for them, the old leaf bracts covering the pseudo bulbs should be carefully removed by splitting and peeling back. The best method of control is to take a small artist's brush dipped in a solution of methylated spirit and to liberally paint the areas suspected of harbouring the pests. Methylated spirits kills the soft, unprotected mealy bug upon contact and its swift penetrating action will find those which remain unseen. Scale insects, particularly the hard, mussel type, must be dislodged to be killed, and the best method of dislodging any visible scale is by scrubbing with an old tooth brush dipped in methylated spirit. This treatment will not harm the base of the plant in any way, but if spirit is used on the leaves they should be immediately washed with clean water. On very soft leaved orchids methylated spirits can cause some burning and it should never be used on flower buds for the same reason. In any case, this should not become necessary as these pests are unlikely to be found on the faster developing flower spikes and buds.

Cultural faults
From the above it can be seen that orchids in the home can very easily be kept clean and free from pests. They are far more likely to suffer from cultural faults. It is difficult to create the conditions required for their good health until an understanding of their needs has been gained through experience. The most common problems arise through mistaken kindness such as overwatering, or placing the orchid in the wrong position in the home where it cannot possibly succeed. The placing of plants is critical and can make all the difference to their well-being.

Light is one of the most important factors of orchid culture in the home, and most orchids should receive plenty of it. However, the plants must not stand in the direct sunlight for any length of time as this will result in scorching of the leaves, particularly with the soft leaved varieties. Scorching will show up as ugly black patches spreading over the area of the leaf receiving the direct sunlight. The remedy is to remove the plant to a shadier position and thus protect it from further burning. The most dangerous time of the year is the spring, when the sun is gaining in power and the plants may still be in the exposed positions they have occupied all winter when trying to gain maximum benefit from the meagre light available. The new growths on the plant which have appeared since the autumn will not be used to bright sunlight, and it is these parts which are most susceptible to burning. For this reason, the plants standing in a window sill with light from one direction only should be placed with their young growths facing into the room, exposing the more mature bulbs and leaves to the light.

The odd patch of burn on a mature leaf can be trimmed back to improve the appearance of the plant, but apart from this action there is no way of removing the disfigurement until the plant grows itself out of it. Those plants which produce a minimum of foliage cannot afford to have their leaves removed and it may be preferable to leave the damaged leaves on the plant. The patches of burn will not spread or cause any further harm to the plant, unless the area becomes infected by bacteria or fungus. This is only likely to occur where conditions of cold or wet persist, which is unlikely indoors.

Overwatering orchids is difficult because of the open, free draining nature of their compost. However, plants potted in the wrong type of compost will very quickly be in trouble from overwatering and suffocation of the roots. Overwatering can arise where a plant has been allowed to stand directly in water, or by too frequent applications of water, particularly when a plant is at rest, causing a sodden condition of the compost which will rot the roots and sometimes cause black fungal spots to appear on the leaves. The loss of the roots will in turn result in shrivelling of the pseudo bulbs which are unable to absorb the moisture in the compost. If the situation remains unchanged, excessive premature loss of foliage will occur. Having reached this stage, the plant will take several years to recover, if at all, and it should be replaced with new stock. However, if it is a favourite orchid which cannot be replaced, it may be worthwhile trying to save the plant by lifting it from its pot and removing all compost and dead roots. A group of leafless bulbs should be divided, and repotted singly for growing as propagations. Plants which have been spotted in time and which have not lost excessive foliage should be repotted after removing the dead roots. With careful nurturing these will be encouraged to make new roots and grow afresh. During this time daily sponging of the foliage will prevent further moisture loss through the leaves, while the compost should remain on the dry side until the new roots can be seen at the base of the leading bulb.

Underwatering is a more frequent complaint of indoor orchids. Due to the openness of their compost, it will dry out far quicker than that of other house plants. The first sign of an underwatered plant is shrivelling of the bulbs, or limp and dull foliage. The remedy is obvious, but in severe cases it may slow their growth or force the plant into a rest at the wrong time which can upset their growth cycle and affect flowering.

Fungal spots can sometimes occur on foliage or flowers due to cultural faults such as overwatering or lack of fresh air, where the plants are growing in an enclosed frame. This condition can occur in greenhouses particularly during the winter months when the balance between the temperature and humidity is upset. Indoors, it may be caused by cold or draughts as well as the causes mentioned above. The marks can be prevented from spreading by the use of a powdered fungicide mixed with a little water to form a paste, and painted onto the affected parts. Obviously, these marks will not disappear without the removal of the leaf, and a new position should be found for the plant while it grows out of the problem.

Another cause of odd markings or blotches on orchid foliage is old age. Most orchids retain their foliage for several years and it is natural that as a leaf ages it will become spotted or affected by black tipping. When this occurs on the oldest leaves, it is nothing to worry about. These old leaves will also turn yellow from time to time and be shed quite naturally by the plant. This is the plant going through its natural cycle of growth and the older leaves have already been replaced by the new growth before they are shed. Deciduous orchids will usually shed all of their foliage as they commence their resting period. Therefore, the loss of foliage can be a normal function for the plant, or a bad cultural fault, depending upon the variety.

Many orchids carry natural markings on their bulbs or leaves. This can take the form of coloured spotting at the base of the plants as with some Paphiopedilums, or speckling on the bulbs and undersides of foliage which occurs particularly in some Odontoglossums. These markings should not be confused with pest damage or cultural faults.

Generally, naturally occurring markings will be observed on the new growth as it appears and will not greatly alter its appearance. They do not appear suddenly, on mature growth, as would a blemish of some kind. Most of these colorations are extremely attractive and enhance the beauty of the plant. For example, the handsome mottling on the foliage of many Paphiopedilums and Phalaenopsis, and the dark purple peppering at the base and on the undersides of their leaves. *Odontoglossum grande* is an example of a species whose foliage is peppered with dark brown on the undersides which often causes concern to beginners. The little red flowered species, *Cryptochilus sanguineus* bears a dark red margin to the leaves on its new growth which is extremely attractive, and a few of the

Cattleya and Oncidium species have heavy, dark red blotches or spots on their bulbs and leaves. Often some of this colouring is carried through to their hybrids.

The most delicate part of any plant is the flower spike and its buds. If conditions are not right, even though the plant has produced a flower spike, the buds will turn yellow and drop off. Apart from insect attacks mentioned earlier, this is most certainly a cultural fault, and one must take a further look at the conditions provided to assess the remedy. Over and underwatering as mentioned will cause bud drop, as will incorrect temperatures. With cool house orchids it may be an indication that they are being grown in too warm a temperature, particularly at night. Where gas is used in the home for heating, fumes from these appliances will very quickly spoil buds. Trouble often occurs when a plant in bud is removed from its growing area and brought into the room for the enjoyment of watching the buds open. It is no use standing a plant in bud on a television set in a dark corner and expecting it to flower. In all probability the buds will drop off without opening. Plants which are to be removed from their growing area to a display area should be left until they are in full flower; at this stage it is safe to move them.

If a plant does not bloom as expected, there may be a number of reasons, all of them cultural. The plant may be weak or sickly through incorrect culture or insect infestation as previously mentioned. If a strong, healthy plant refuses to bloom it may be lack of sufficient light, or too warm a temperature. The latter will result in a beautiful green, healthy plant with growth that is too lush. A harder growth must be produced with lower temperatures which is more likely to bloom. With correct treatment all orchids should bloom annually, and many of the modern hybrids will bloom more frequently.

Damage

Accidental damage to plants is more likely to occur in the home than outside or in the greenhouse, especially where there are pets or young children about. A plant which is knocked over may be injured in some way. The plant which has merely come loose from its pot needs nothing more than firming down by tapping on the floor, and will be none the worse for the experience. Broken leaves can be removed for appearance, provided that the plant will not miss them. A broken Cymbidium leaf for example, can easily be removed without notice, while a Phalaenopsis with a cracked leaf will require drying and dusting with sulphur to prevent the damage from spreading. The elongated bulbs of Dendrobiums and

Cattleyas can all too easily become snapped midway if they fall over. Again sulphur should be applied to the exposed end of the bulb and the plant kept on the dry side until it is well healed. New growth will commence from the base provided this is undamaged.

Index of Genera, Species and Hybrids

Numbers in *italics* refer to pages containing illustrations.

89